Rising to the Challenge:

The Transition Movement and People of Faith

Praise for *Rising to the Challenge*

Rising to the Challenge *is a beautiful book about a beautiful movement. Almost by definition, hoping we can effect a transition is a statement of faith, which means that those of us in communities of faith should be emboldened to support this great work with everything we've got.*
— **Bill McKibben**, author of The Comforting Whirlwind: God, Job, and the Scale of Creation

Working on climate change issues every day, I frequently hear individuals lament that they don't know what to do or they can never do enough to meet the challenge. Many people are overwhelmed by the daunting spectre of a radically changing world, with severe storms and drought, rising sea level, resource wars and escalating conflict becoming the norm. The Transition movement provides a package of inspiring ideas for what to do and connects people so they do not have to do this alone. It is what Gandhi called "constructive program" — building the kind of community that both your heart and your head tell you is needed. Thanks to Ruah for giving us a compelling summary of the movement and exploring the role of the faith community in bringing about our transition to renewable energy and a holistic, spirit-centered society.

— **Shelley Tanenbaum**, General Secretary, Quaker Earthcare Witness

Can rising awareness of climate change help usher in a more peaceful, equitable, and environmentally sound future? Can it help unite people across diverse religious and philosophical traditions? Quaker environmental leader Ruah Swennerfelt thinks so, and has now shared her personal journey toward that hopeful understanding. Ruah chronicles her involvement in the worldwide Transition Town movement, visiting Transition communities and forward-looking permaculture projects across the U.S., Europe, Brazil, and Israel/Palestine. Drawing on the lived experiences of key founders and an impressive variety of on-the-ground organizers, she offers a highly accessible and compelling account of Transition's practical and visionary dimensions, and reveals how the wisdom of diverse faith traditions has helped inspire this uniquely forward-looking and community-centered movement.

— **Brian Tokar**, Lecturer in Environmental Studies at the University of Vermont, author of The Green Alternative, Earth for Sale, and Toward Climate Justice: Perspectives on the Climate Crisis and Social Change

Rising to the Challenge *is a strong call to respond to the global climate challenge and put faith into action to "see what love can do." Swennerfelt draws on inspiring stories from the world's experimentation crucibles in Transition, offering up her vision of radical dreaming. Here we learn about energy descent planning, repair cafés, and permaculture communities, and the important role of faith traditions in healing the world. Based on her travels to Transition Towns around the world, this book demonstrates the possibilities of practicing loving kindness on a global scale. It is a marvelous manifesto for resilience and a powerful testimony of hope, reflecting Swenerfelt's own deep personal commitment, an inspiring voice in this time of transformation.*
— **Stephanie Kaza**, author of *Hooked! Buddhist Essays on Greed, Desire and the Urge to Consume*

It is always a beautiful gift when someone introduces two of her close friends, knowing that a pair of strangers have much to offer to each other. In this short book, Ruah Swennerfelt performs that act of hospitality on an institutional level, providing a heartfelt introduction between the 10-year-old Transition Town Movement and long-standing faith traditions. Drawing on stories from many countries and many faiths, she reveals common perspectives and shared goals for these two movements, both of which are seeking to make a difference in the world. As an environmental activist on the faith side, I have been blessed by her insights, information, and her hope for this new collaboration.
— **Reverend Peter Sawtell**,[1] Executive Director Eco-Justice Ministries

The seeds of sanity are sprouting — *and at the grass roots, more than grass is growing! Ruah Swennerfelt's book not only shares some of the many sprouts of the great turning, the transition to an Earth we actually share with all life-forms — but itself sows seeds in every reader.*
— **Rabbi Arthur Waskow**,[2] director of The Shalom Center, author of *Down-to-Earth Judaism* and co-author of *Freedom Journeys*

Rising to the Challenge *is a book full of hope and optimism. Swennerfelt looks at the Transition Movement, which encourages people to band together with neighbors to design a transition to a low-carbon future. She examines the role of faith in the movement, and the ways in which the Transition Movement might strengthen and enliven faith communities. Beautifully written, personal and inspiring, the book points a way forward out of despair to connection and action rooted in deep connection to the sacredness of Earth.*
— **Starhawk**,[3] author of *The Empowerment Manual: A Guide for Collaborative Groups* and *Truth or Dare: Encounters with Power, Authority, and Mystery*

QIF Focus Books[4]

1—*Fueling our Future*: *A Dialogue about Technology, Ethics, Public Policy, and Remedial Action,* coordinated by Ed Dreby and Keith Helmuth, edited by Judy Lumb, 2009.

2—*How on Earth Do We Live Now? Natural Capital, Deep Ecology, and the Commons,* by David Ciscel, Barbara Day, Keith Helmuth, Sandra Lewis, and Judy Lumb, 2011.

3—*Genetically Modified Crops: Promises, Perils, and the Need for Public Policy,* by Anne Mitchell, with Pinayur Rajagopal, Keith Helmuth, and Susan Holtz, 2011.

4—*How Does Societal Transformation Happen? Values Development, Collective Wisdom, and Decision Making for the Common Good,* by Leonard Joy, 2011.

5—*It's the Economy, Friends: Understanding the Growth Dilemma,* edited by Ed Dreby, Keith Helmuth, and Margaret Mansfield, 2012.

6—*Beyond the Growth Dilemma: Toward an Ecologically Integrated Economy,* edited by Ed Dreby and Judy Lumb, 2012.

7—*A Quaker Approach to Research: Collaborative Practice and Communal Discernment,* by Gray Cox, with Charles Blanchard, Geoff Garver, Keith Helmuth, Leonard Joy, Judy Lumb, and Sara Wolcott, 2014.

8—*Climate, Food and Violence: Understanding the Connections, Exploring Responses,* by Judy Lumb, Phil Emmi, Mary Gilbert, Laura Holliday, Leonard Joy, and Shelley Tanenbaum, 2014.

9—*Toward a Right Relationship with Finance: Debt, Interest, Growth, and Security,* by Pamela Haines, Ed Dreby, David Kane, and Charles Blanchard, 2016.

10—*Rising to the Challenge: The Transition Movement and People of Faith,* by Ruah Swennerfelt, 2016.

Rising to the Challenge:
The Transition Movement and People of Faith

Ruah Swennerfelt

Foreword by Rob Hopkins

Front Cover: March in Rome in support of the Pope's Encyclical, June 27, 2015 (*photo by Hoda Baraka <hodabaraka.com> used with permission*)

Back Cover: Participants in Contemplation
(*photo courtesy Deposit Photos <depositphotos.com>*)

QIF Focus Book 10
Quaker Institute for the Future 2016

Published by *Producciones de la Hamaca,* Caye Caulker, Belize
<producciones-hamaca.com> for the Quaker Institute for the Future.
ISBN: 978-976-8142-92-4 (print edition)
ISBN: 978-976-8142-91-7 (e-book edition)
Rising to the Challenge is the tenth in the series of *QIF Focus Books*
ISBN: 978-976-8142-90-0
(formerly *Quaker Institute for the Future Pamphlets*)

This book was printed on-demand by Lightning Source, Inc. (LSI). The on-demand printing system is environmentally friendly because books are printed as needed, instead of in large numbers that might end up in someone's basement or a dump site. In addition, LSI is committed to using materials obtained by sustainable forestry practices. LSI is certified by Sustainable Forestry Initiative (SFI® Certificate Number: PwC-SFICOC-345 SFI-00980). The Sustainable Forestry Initiative is an independent, internationally recognized non-profit organization responsible for the SFI certification standard, the world's largest single-forest certification standard. The SFI program is based on the premise that responsible environmental behavior and sound business decisions can co-exist to the benefit of communities, customers and the environment, today and for future generations <sfiprogram.org>.

QIF Focus Books aim to provide critical information and understanding born of careful discernment on social, economic, and ecological realities, inspired by the testimonies and values of the Religious Society of Friends (Quakers). We live in a time when social and ecological issues are converging toward catastrophic breakdown. Human adaptation to social, economic and planetary realities must be re-thought and re-designed. **QIF Focus Books** are dedicated to this calling, based on a spiritual and ethical commitment to "right relationship" with Earth's whole commonwealth of life.   <quakerinstitute.org>

Producciones de la Hamaca is dedicated to:

—Celebration and documentation of Earth
    and all her inhabitants,
—Restoration and conservation of Earth's
    natural resources,
—Creative expression of the sacredness of
    Earth and Spirit.

Table of Contents

Foreword

His Holiness the Dalai Lama, when asked about the differences between the world's faiths, usually chooses instead to focus on what they have in common. "The purpose of all the major religious traditions is not to construct big temples on the outside, but to create temples of goodness and compassion inside, in our hearts," he says.

In 2004 I had my climate change dark night of the soul. The urgency, the imperative nature and scale of what we have to do, and the precariousness of what we could so easily lose, really landed within me. It wasn't a good place to be. When I emerged from the other side, and began the process of piecing together what we now call Transition, one of the key questions for me was, "What would a compassionate response to climate change look like?"

What would it look like, I wondered, if we saw climate change as a remarkable gift, as our opportunity to practice loving kindness on a vast scale, to design an approach that started at the community scale and went on to inspire a shift at all levels, which brought us closer together rather than driving us further apart? It is this question of what a compassionate response could look like that has driven me since the Transition began.

Here in the UK, sociologists talk about there being "an epidemic of loneliness". An epidemic of loneliness. For the dysfunctional economists, planners and advisors who drive our economy ever onwards, that is considered an entirely acceptable side-effect of progress. But we can already see in the projects and activities emerging through the Transition movement that it is perfectly possible to create an economy that makes us healthier, better connected and happier.

A study of the Bristol Pound (the local currency in which the city's Mayor takes his full salary) found that people using the currency had substantially more conversations than those that didn't. A Repair Café run by the Transition group in Pasadena, California, offers to repair anything for free. The only trade required is that while the repair takes place, you sit in a chair opposite the fixer and tell them a story about your life.

Transition Town Media in Pennsylvania opened a Free Store, but they see it, rather than as being about the goods, or the trade, as being a "compassion-building exercise". In Brussels, Belgium, in a community best known as a red-light district, families have created a food garden in the street, and have found that for the first time ever, people stop and talk to each other, children come out to play, a community begins to meet itself.

In London, a member of Transition Kensal to Kilburn reads a story about an elderly woman who died and whose body lay undiscovered for six years, leading him to wonder, on his busy London street, if he died, who might notice? In response, and inspired by noting grapes growing in neighbouring streets and by meeting an 80-year-old Italian man, he kicked off the "Unthinkable Drinkable" project, which resulted in everyone on his street coming out and taking it in turns to tread wine in the traditional manner. As they readily admit, the resultant wine, "NW6" (the area's postcode), was "borderline undrinkable", but in reality they have fermented, created, initiated something far more important. In the same way, what was the garden project in Brussels really growing? What was the Repair Café really repairing?

Rising to the Challenge: The Transition Movement and People of Faith by Ruah Swennerfelt is a hugely important contribution to the growing literature on Transition. Since its inception, Transition has taken itself in many unexpected directions, has continually surprised us, has popped up, like mushrooms in an autumn field, sometimes in places we expected it to, and sometimes where we really didn't expect it to. The interest of the world of faith communities, initially reflected in Tim Gorringe and Rosie Beckham's book, *The Transition Movement for Churches: A Prophetic Imperative for Today,* has been one of those unexpected, yet delightful, developments. *Rising to the Challenge* takes it to another level, and has done us a great service. It does what Transition does so beautifully, it seeks common ground.

I am often heard to say that the building of common ground is one of the great tasks of our times, putting our own egos, positions, familiarities to one side in the interests of finding common ground. Mahasiddha Machig Lhadbron, an eleventh-century Tibetan mystic, wrote:

"To realise the essence of consciousness...

Approach what you find repulsive

Help whoever you think you cannot help.

Let go of anything you are attached to

Go to places that scare you.

Be mindful!"[5]

It is advice that is as useful when working to build community resilience, as when trying to realise the essence of consciousness. While those rooted in activism tend to feel drawn to doing, to rolling their sleeves up and making projects happen, those rooted in faith can also bring tools and insights rooted in being. An area that distinguishes Transition from other similar community-led approaches is, I think, the focus it gives to the inner life of groups, to the need to factor in personal resilience. It recognises that there is no point trying to replace the current way in which our culture and our economy works by pushing for an alternative but trying to get there by behaving in the same ways as what we're trying to change.

In Transition, great care is taken to ensure that groups know how to run successful meetings, how to resolve conflict, how to design meetings that people will actually look forward to going to, to the observation that how a project is done is as important as what the project itself achieves. And this in turn requires creating spaces for stillness, for reflection, for listening, something faith groups have been doing for more than just a little longer than Transition groups.

I think that as well as an environmental case for Transition, we are also building a case for its being a public health and wellbeing strategy. We know that acting more compassionately has beneficial impacts on the people around us, it can be infectious, it can make us healthier and more able to resist disease, it can generate more pro-environmental behaviour and it helps us overcome depression. When done well, Transition creates numerous invitations for people to act kindly, to act compassionately, to connect with others in a world that increasingly isolates us.

Just as Transition focuses on the art of finding and nurturing common ground with those around us, so this book focuses on finding and nurturing common ground between faiths, common ground that could yield so very much in our pursuit of a stable climate and more resilient world. While it is important that Transition itself is not co-opted by any particular faith or spiritual perspective, and remains open and inviting to as many people as possible, it offers, as this book shows, a powerful tool for faith groups to come together around.

So thank you Ruah, thanks to everyone whose stories appear in these pages, and may this book prove to be the catalyst that it deserves to be.

Rob Hopkins[6]
Transition Network

Preface

As a New England Quaker active in the Transition Movement, I know from personal experience that being an active participant in a local Transition initiative can be a meaningful spiritual practice of healing and repairing the world. Faithful Jews have long referred to this healing practice by the Hebrew phrase, "*tikkun 'olam.*" My spiritual life, as well as my knowledge and effectiveness as a community organizer, have deepened and grown since I became involved in the Transition Town Movement. I believe that many other people of faith in the United States and elsewhere can have a similar experience.

This book is intended to be a tool for those already involved in greening their faith traditions and for those who see green faith as part of a sustainable human presence on planet Earth. Both groups feel the need for communities that have cohesion and resilience and find that working through Transition at the grassroots builds those kinds of communities. Those just coming to understand that care for Earth is a spiritual concern can learn more about what they can do. Everyone will find stories from people around the world who have found a home in the Transition Movement. This book is designed to be useful to local Transition organizers who do not see themselves as religious, but who want to better understand how to reach out to, and interact with, communities of faith in their local areas. These insights should help Transition organizers build stronger, more inclusive Transition Initiatives by drawing on the institutional, ethical, and motivational resources of local faith communities.

I am a faith-based Transition organizer, not an academic theologian. So while each chapter is spiritually and theologically informed, this book has an eclectic, movement-building bent to it. I am writing this book for a multi-faith audience, not just a Christian one, because this diverse community-organizing Movement brings together—by design—people of many faiths, their secular neighbors, and the many people in our country who self-identify as "spiritual, but not religious." This book explores what people of faith can bring to this innovative Movement and how the Transition Movement is also consistent with long-standing religious testimonies, scriptures, and traditions. It is filled with stories and hands-on instruction for building a Transition Movement that is both fun and a creative way to foster local communities that are environmentally sustainable, socially just, and spiritually fulfilling.

I have attempted to combine important information for the readers with very personal stories—my own as well as those gathered near and far over the last six years.

In the Introduction I share my story of how I came to embrace the Transition Movement and its ideals, and my reflections on my experience. I hope that this will illuminate how personal faith journeys can motivate people to engage in building ever more beloved communities in their neighborhoods, cities, and regions through the Transition Movement.

Chapter 1 includes an introduction to our global predicament and signs of hope from people of faith.

Chapter 2 describes permaculture, out of which Transition arose, and chronicles the beginnings of Transition through the spiritual journeys of Transition co-founders Rob Hopkins and Naresh Giangrande, and Steve Chase, an early Transition organizer and contributor to this book.

Chapter 3 describes the Transition Movement, its emergence, vision, growth, and stages of organizing.

Chapter 4 tells some local organizing stories and interesting accomplishments of the Transition Movement from many places around the world. These examples of Transition in practice are gathered from the published literature on the Transition Movement, phone interviews, and my own extended Transition study trip through Israel, Palestine, Europe, and North America in 2011.

Chapter 5 is based on extensive interviewing of people of faith who are already active in the Transition Town Movement.

Chapter 6 looks at the evolving ideas behind the Transition Town Movement, especially how Transition members are increasingly rising to the challenge of finding creative ways to build up a new, non-corporate, re-localized, resilient, and community-based economy, with opportunities for all.

The Endnotes give details of sources and additional information. A List of Interviews is included. The Bibliography includes books, magazines, and films that have inspired me and will help anyone wanting to rise to the challenge and explore the Transition Movement further—and I hope you will!

The concept of "peak oil" was very important to the co-founders of the Transition Movement and to others who have joined the Movement, so the term "peak oil" appears in this book because it inspired their actions. Today that term is not used very much.

Climate change, climate disruption, climate chaos, and climate justice are additional terms we use to describe why we are concerned and why we are motivated to change to a renewable energy future.

Nevertheless, peak oil is still an issue. More oil is available deep in the earth, but it becomes more difficult and dangerous to extract, as seen in deep-water oil extraction, tar sands oil, and fracking. The decreasing net energy obtained for the energy used to extract the oil makes the process less and less practical or profitable. The recent campaign by activists around the world to "leave it in the ground" indicates that we need to stop burning fossil fuels to assure the planet is habitable for future generations of all life.

In many books the author uses last names when referring to another author or interviewee. I have chosen to use the last name when I don't know the person. But if I have had some personal experience of a person, I have used their first name, which seems more personal and in sync with the intimacy of the Transition Movement.

Ruah Swennerfelt[7]
March 2016

Acknowledgements

A number of years ago, Steve Chase and I were interviewed by a Quaker-run radio program. The moderator asked us to talk about our experiences with the Transition Town Movement. As we talked, we recognized that we were kindred souls on a path to healing the negative effects of human-caused climate change. When I was approached to write this book I naturally turned to Steve to help me. I consider him a major contributor, and I want to publicly appreciate his assistance and acknowledge that many of his ideas and his words are incorporated herein.

Of course I appreciate the groundbreakers in the Transition Movement—Rob Hopkins, Naresh Giangrande, and Sophie Banks. They had the courage to engage a town with their seemingly wild ideas, and they've continued to shape and nurture the Movement as it's grown beyond their hopes and dreams. I especially want to thank Rob for taking time out of a very busy Transition conference to be interviewed by an unknown devotee. His generosity, genuineness, humility, and good humor are endearing. He has also taken the time to write this book's foreword in the midst of his own writing and involvement in the Transition.

And since this journey of writing a book started with my belonging to a Transition Initiative, I very much appreciate my fellow Transition Town travelers in Charlotte, Vermont, where I live. They bring their own creativity and heart and soul to the work. I feel supported and cared for by them.

I'm also grateful to all the people who were willing to be interviewed, those included here and those whose words didn't find their way into this book. They were inspiring and so much fun to be with.

And I'm grateful to those who walk their talk and have taken time in their busy lives to add their endorsements to the book—Stephanie Kaza, Bill McKibben, the Reverend Peter Sawtell, Starhawk, Shelley Tanenbaum, Brian Tokar, and Rabbi Arthur Waskow. Special thanks go to Rabbi Waskow for invaluable comments and criticisms that have helped this book become more inviting to a multi-faith audience. And I can't thank Bill McKibben enough for his foresight, earnestness, and tenacity in bringing the issues of climate change to people all around the planet. I feel blessed!

I want to send my heartfelt thank-you to the folks of the Quaker Institute for the Future (QIF). Their support for the development of this project has been terrific, especially the assistance from Judy Lumb and Dorothy Beveridge of *Producciones de la Hamaca,* and Barbara Day, QIF's venerable proofeader. I am very proud to have this book take its place as one of the *QIF Focus Books,* which provide critical information and understanding on social, economic, and ecological realities, inspired by the testimonies and values of the Religious Society of Friends.

Last but not least, I am so thankful for Louis Cox, my husband, partner, and best friend, who patiently read and re-read the chapters, giving sound editorial suggestions, with patience and enthusiasm. He has been a faithful part of Transition Town Charlotte, and has supported me in my quest to learn more, which sometimes took me away from him for months. Our journey together over the last 21 years has been a thrill, and I look forward to where it takes us next.

Ruah Swennerfelt[7]
March 2016

Yoav Egozi and Noel Longhurst's workshop on
"How Change Happens" at Seale Hayne, Newton Abbot, Devon, U.K.
(photo by Mike Grenville)

INTRODUCTION
MY JOURNEY TO TRANSITION

My spiritual path to Transition organizing goes back to my finding the Religious Society of Friends in 1975. As a single mother of three, I was searching for a caring community where my children would learn good values. The Quaker testimonies of simplicity, peace, integrity, community, and equality guided us through their growing years. Like many Quakers throughout history, I became active in peace and justice issues, and was led to risk arrest to resist the U.S. government policy of sending arms to El Salvador. I served several jail terms for this peace work. I believe there are times when we must take a stand on behalf of peoples' struggles for justice, regardless of the price.

My Quaker tradition includes the possibility of "continuing revelation." I experienced this first-hand one day in 1991, at a world conference of Friends in Honduras. While there, I picked up a Quaker Earthcare Witness (QEW) booklet by Elizabeth G. Watson, and her quote from QEW member Mary Ann Percy leapt out at me: "There's no peace without a planet."[8]

That simple statement changed my life. I began to see how all social and ecological issues are interconnected, and that to continue to work for peace I also needed to work for a healthy planet. When I joined QEW shortly thereafter, I began to appreciate that a healthy planet means integrity for all of Creation, not just the "resources" that are currently appropriated—and only dimly understood—by industrial civilization. My role in QEW was to help spread this awareness more widely among the larger Quaker movement. The other part of my experience of continuing revelation was personal—examining my own ecological footprint and making significant efforts to reduce it.

1

In the 1990s, I got very serious about this peace-with-Earth commitment. It started with my moving into a hand-built, off-grid, solar-powered house in the country. It continued in 1995, when Louis Cox and I, having met through our work with QEW, joined lives. We inspired each other to live more "sustainably" and to set a good example for others. We have worked hard to minimize our dependence on a private automobile by car-pooling and working at home. We have grown a lot of our own food, heated with wood harvested from our land, worked with hand tools, and bought second-hand goods whenever possible. Our household's demand for electricity has been the most challenging part of this. With New England's typical cloudy weather and short winter days, we have had to add solar panels and devise ways to get more power from them, as well as conserve energy.

These are all values that I still hold deeply. Nevertheless, my ecological footprint has remained large by world standards. Deep down I have had to face an uncomfortable truth: Even though I am still using only a fraction of the resources consumed by a typical North American household, my lifestyle cannot be considered sustainable. This led me to look for new and different approaches — ones that emphasized community and institutional solutions beyond what I was doing or not doing as an individual homeowner. I was increasingly seeing the need for a more radical response to environmental degradation than just individuals trying to live a bit more simply in the midst of an unsustainable, polluting, oil-dependent world.

I embraced the permaculture ideals and took a course to become a permaculture designer. The course I took was unique. It was titled, "Earth Activist Training," and was led by Starhawk, a spiritual leader among neo-pagans worldwide. I have attempted to live by the permaculture principles in my day-to-day life, recognizing that they guide more than the way I grow my food. They guide the way I live on the land and how I relate to my community.

I was a co-founder of Vermont Interfaith Power & Light organization (VTIPL). I hold onto hope when I regularly participate in VTIPL Board meetings, where I learn that so many faith communities are making significant changes in their energy use. It is exciting to collaborate in this multi-faith organization, as we find common languages and understandings to address the climate crisis.

Becoming a Local Organizer

I was struck by an illustration in the November 2012 issue of *National Geographic* of a proposed three-mile-wide solar collector that would circle Earth as a satellite. It would be made up of 240,000 replaceable photovoltaic panels. That is a lot of effort and capital — a lot of eggs put into one basket — to secure enough electricity to maintain current affluent lifestyles! Would it be worth the risk and cost? — I don't think so. Since all sustainable energy ultimately comes from the sun, the question is whether industrial-scale, centralized systems can serve our needs better than working together to "relocalize," that is, to make community-based and decentralized economies. In response to this insight, I have become a local organizer.

That all started about 15 years ago, when my town's conservation commission formed reading and study groups, using the Northwest Earth Institute's series of study guides. Ours was one of several groups who decided, after a few years, that we needed to be doing more than reading and talking. So, with others in the town, we formed the Charlotte Sustainable Living Network (CSLN). For several years we showed documentary videos, invited speakers, hosted local-food potlucks, and generally raised awareness in our town about sustainability issues. Then I learned about the Transition Town Movement at a QEW annual gathering. I was so impressed with the hope that the Movement offered that I attended a weekend Transition Training workshop. Inspired by the people and ideas I encountered at that workshop, I shared what I had learned with the CSLN group. After our group had explored the Transition-US website and read Rob Hopkins's book, *The Transition Handbook*, we were led to change our name to Transition Town Charlotte.

When Charlotte became a Transition Town, we also became part of a worldwide movement, working towards resilience. "Resilience" seemed to us to describe much better than "sustainability" what is needed as a community starts to confront unprecedented challenges in the areas of energy, economics, and environment. Sustainability was defined in too many ways, and the word was losing its efficacy as a goal. Too many people thought of it as finding ways to continue business as usual. Resilience, on the other hand, means the ability to weather the likely and possible social, environmental, and economic storms that lie ahead. It means strengthening community networks, learning what strengths and weaknesses are a part of our community. It means learning what human and natural resources

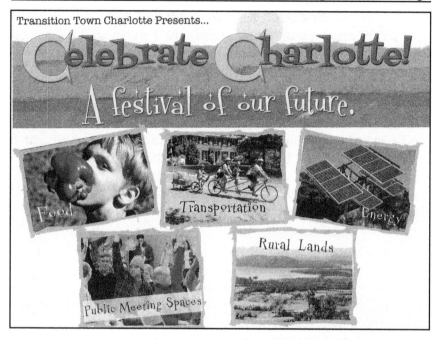

Transition Town Charlotte Board: (*from left*) Dora Coates, Tiny Sikkes, Nancy Severance, Louis Cox, Carol Blanshine, Rebecca Foster, Suzy Hodgson, Bud Shriner, Amos Baehr, Catherine Bock, Wolfger Schneider. *Not present:* Margaret Woodruff, Mike Yantachka, Cathy Hunter, and Abby Foulk.

(*photo by Ruah Swennerfelt*)

are available to us locally in times of need. The Transition Movement is full of possibility. It doesn't dwell on the negative, though educating ourselves about the world situation continues to be important. It focuses instead on the positive.

Not long ago a few of us were asking ourselves how we might redefine our lives, personally and in our communities, to address the many crises of the planet and live within its ecological limits. Many people I know have begun moving in that direction, but it is not happening fast enough. Sometimes I look around in a public place and wonder how in the world we are going to get all those people to embrace the changes that would make their lives more resilient. Is it possible to build a movement that captures the hearts of millions, as happened in the Civil Rights Movement? Can we somehow motivate the wider population to consume and drive less, eat locally, live more frugally, and un-plug? What will motivate them?

Even though the disruptions looming before us could send me to hide under my bed covers, I get up each day with hope. This is because I regularly join with others in my town, in my faith community, in my state, in my country, and occasionally with others in the world, to try to make a difference. I get up with hope because Transition Town Charlotte held a workshop about keeping poultry and more than 40 people showed up, right here in our little town of about 4,500 people. It was a lively and fun event, and maybe it motivated a few more people to think about developing a strong local economy. I am hopeful because at my Friends Meeting some of us were discussing Bill McKibben's book, *Eaarth, Making a Life on a Tough New Planet,* and it led us to explore ways to make significant heart-based changes within our Meeting community.

Although all this work with my town might be considered secular work, my faith informs my actions. My faith guides me to care for those in need or for a suffering planet. Though I had worked for peace and justice before awakening to the environmental issues facing our culture, I still had a strong sense of our connectedness to all of life. As a Quaker, I have to ask whether I can possibly live out the Quaker Testimonies of simplicity, peace, integrity, community, equality, and sustainability without acting in the world where there is a need. I bring my Quaker faith into my work with Transition, without always naming it. I was especially drawn by the movement's emphasis on Inner Transition. Real change springs from the heart, though I recognize that the effort to change the laws and regulations is also important. My experience with Vermont

Interfaith Power & Light confirms that all faiths have a foundation in living a just life.

I have been inspired by Erik Andrus and Erica Hurwitz, a couple who own Bound Brook Farm in Vergennes, Vermont, only a few miles from where we live. Erik and Erica's dream was to grow wheat, partly to supply Erik's start-up bakery and partly to sell in the Champlain Valley. Erik started a CSA (Community Supported Agriculture), specializing in the sale of breads, croissants, and other mouth-watering delights at local farmers markets. His goal of a net-zero-energy farm is assisted by his use of draft horses. What Erik did not know about the land he purchased in 2005 was that a large portion of it is not well drained and therefore is not good for wheat farming. Pulling up stakes was not an option after all the labor to build the house, the wood-fired oven, and other essentials for the bakery. So Erik is learning to adapt to the land he has.

Erik discovered another niche to fill in the Champlain Valley, where so many people are focused on eating locally. That niche was rice. He explained it this way to *The Burlington Free Press*:

> "I love bread, and I love beer more than I love a plate of brown rice and a glass of sake — but if my inclination says bread, and the land says rice, I have to listen to what the land says."[9]

With that said, he invested money and time for his first rice harvest, and he is hoping to produce 4,000 pounds a year. The rice is harvested with a horse-drawn reaper binder, and after the drying and threshing it is processed with a rice huller that Erik ordered from China. Recently Louis and I went to a rice harvest party at the farm and picked up our pre-ordered brown and white rice in lovely cloth bags. We got a tour of the rice paddies and enjoyed time with others supporting the farm. This experience of purchasing food close to home and knowing the growers and producers is an exceptional treat. It is a connection that is priceless.

I was very moved by Erik's statement about listening to the land. How brilliant, I thought, to truly understand the land where you live, to have a deep sense of place! That's what permaculture is essentially about. How often in human history have we not listened to what the land says? Semi-arid lands turned into deserts through excessive irrigation and wildlife habitats destroyed by urban sprawl are just two examples of how our vaunted human creativity has often backfired. What would it be like if we all took the time to observe and listen to the place where we live? Observation is one of the basic principles of permaculture. Once you really know your place—observe where the sun shines on the land in all seasons, know the changing temperatures, and observe how the natural world adapts to the place—it's then time to grow your food.

My spiritual journey to Transition has been informed by my experiences on the land where I live and by the examples of people like Erik and Erica. It has been shaped by Friends' faith and practice and by the many lives well lived by Friends. I was lucky to meet so many wonderful people working for a sustainable planet, especially those in Quaker Earthcare Witness, with whom I had the privilege of working for 17 years.

Today I want to be an agent for healing for the planet, for the future, for my life, for my children, for my grandchildren, and for my great-grandson. I see climate change right in my backyard, with longer growing seasons and insect pests moving north that are threatening the trees in the Northeast, and with record-breaking high temperatures on Christmas Eve. I read of the vulnerable peoples of the world living near the sea whose homes, lives and cultures are threatened with rising sea levels. I see the heartbreaking photos of polar bears that are losing the sea-ice cover they need to exist. The list is long and my faith urges me to do everything I can to make a difference.

Traveling in Search of Transition

I wake up each day grateful for the beauty of Earth and for the possibilities for love and care that abound. But I know that beyond the daily, personal challenges that we face, there is suffering that can be averted by human intervention. And this motivates me to act on behalf of all that live on Earth. We must do more than feed, clothe, and house the poor. We must change the very systems that cause the great inequity that abounds around the globe. We must do more than save small parcels of land for wildlife and agriculture. We must change the very systems that every day destroy the forests and prime agricultural land and allow the extinctions of species. So, I have journeyed to find ways to change those systems, and when it took me to Transition I was motivated to act because of my belief in the goodness that dwells in the universe.

As I became more involved in the Transition Movement I wanted to learn more about the motivations that drew so many people into it. I visited Transition Towns in the U.S. and helped a few people start Transition Initiatives. But most of the existing Initiatives were in Europe and, although I have a commitment to

reduce my air travel, I believed what I might learn would be beneficial to others. So, with the help of a generous grant from Quaker
Earthcare Witness, I was able to visit Transition Initiatives in Europe
over a four-month period in 2011. Once in Europe I chose to travel
by train, bus, and ferry to reduce my travel carbon footprint. The
timing worked for me to be able to attend the All-France Transition
Conference and the annual International Transition Conference in
England. Through Italy, Spain, France, Ireland, England, Scotland,
Belgium, Netherlands, and Sweden I met with many enthusiastic
Transition participants and visited various projects.

When planning my Transition trip, I wanted to take advantage of the opportunity of my being in Europe to travel north to
Sweden where I was born. I still have quite a few relatives there
and enjoy spending time with them. So I was pleased when I found
a Transition Initiative in Alingsås, a city of about 40,000 people,
where one of my cousins lived!

I also took the opportunity to travel to Israel and Palestine. My
cousin, Harvey Chalfin, whom I had never met, lives in Tiberius,
and it was probably a once-in-a lifetime chance to meet him and
his family. I also visited kibbutzim where good environmental
work was being done. 1 met with an Israeli Arab in his town of
Sakhnin, and saw his project of learning what crops could survive
only on rainwater, since the Israel government denied them irrigation water. I was excited to go to the West Bank to meet Murad
Al Khuffash, a Palestinian farmer involved with permaculture. A
very nervous Harvey drove an excited me to the arranged meeting spot. Murad jumped into our car, having been brought there
by a taxi. And then we drove into Marda, a small village near the
very large, and illegal, Israeli settlement of Ariel, one of the many
disputed Jewish settlements in the West Bank. My report on that
visit is in chapter 2. What a gift it was to meet family and people
doing incredible work! What I learned first-hand during that trip to
Europe and Israel/Palestine is reported in this book.

Throughout my journey I was blessed by the kindness of those
that I met. They took time to meet with me, invited me in to their
homes, and often fed and housed me. A time I remember well with
tenderness is my visit to Transition Kinsale, where much of the
inspiration for the Transition Movement began. During the over-
night ferry ride from France to Ireland we encountered a severe
storm. I had booked only seating instead of a sleeping birth, and
most of us in the second-class section found room on the floor to

sleep. The storm kept me up and I began to get very seasick. Upon arrival in Dublin I rushed to catch a bus for a several-hour ride to Kinsale that exacerbated my seasickness from the closed space and movement of the bus. So, when I arrived at my destination I was not feeling well at all. My four hosts, Klaus, Liz, Hilda, and Jeannie, took pity on me and gently cared for me to revive me enough for dinner and conversation. I'm forever grateful to them.

Wherever I visited I saw the Transition vision growing. There was a common desire for green space, more vegetable gardens, better transportation, and support for bicyclists. I saw the deep need for community, for collaboration, for an opportunity to feel needed, for a chance to make a difference, for a chance to explore ideas, and for a chance to laugh, and sing, and dance.

I am obviously entranced by Transition, but I have a lingering concern that the environmental movement has been primarily a white, middle-class movement. Although Transition calls for inclusion and diversity, it is still a challenge to really be diverse. It is important to avoid inserting one's own vision and ideas too strongly, to refrain from inviting people into "my/our" movement, but instead invite people to be part of a growing movement that needs everyone's input. Transition has that built into its training, but often we get excited and begin to "own" the organization.

I face each day with hope and a smile because I know that my examples are multiplied a million times around the world and that there is a movement that may help turn the tide away from our self-destruction.

When I visited the Transition folks in 2011, I was not on a quest to find out how their faith led them to the Movement, though I recognized that spirit was very alive in the movement through the Inner Transition work and the Heart and Soul groups. I wanted to find out what drew them and what sustained them. But on further reflection I was really curious about the people of faith who were involved in the movement. I wondered where the connection between faith and action lived in the Movement.

I am inspired by the current trend where, instead of working as part of a single congregation or a single denomination, people of faith are working in the wider ecumenical and interfaith communities, and, ultimately, working in the larger movement of movements discussed so well by Paul Hawken in his book, *Blessed Unrest*. Each of these different levels of organizing is important, and needed, but in this book I especially want to encourage people of faith to expand their concept of neighbor and to work closely together with others in a movement that includes members of the interfaith community, people who identify as secular, and people who identify as "spiritual, but not religious." I believe that it is important "to cooperate lovingly with all who share our hopes for the future of the earth."[10]

How might this be done? For me, the loosely organized effort often referred to as the Transition Town Movement, or Transition Movement, is one of the most promising signs I see of humanity rising to the challenge to build beloved communities in an unsustainable and changing world. The Transition Movement is open to people of different faiths and outlooks in our local communities and in national and global networks that support creative local organizing.

I offer this book as a pathway that would strongly attract many people of faith, with the conviction that people of faith want to make a difference and will find it inspiring and helpful to learn more about this international Transition Town Movement, and perhaps even become active in it. In the meantime, I believe that efforts such as the Transition Town Movement, which is spreading around the globe, and Interfaith Power & Light, which is spreading across the U.S., are good places to put our energy. We must work in our communities to educate, re-skill, and energize everyone around us. This is work that is faithful and offers us a joyful way to heal and repair the world several communities at a time. We have to rise to the challenge of holding onto hope in the face of continuing destruction of life on the planet. We have to act, and act now. As the Transition Network website puts it:

"We are living in an age of unprecedented change, with a number of crises converging. Climate change, global economic instability, overpopulation, erosion of community, declining biodiversity, and resource wars, have all stemmed from the availability of cheap, non-renewable fossil fuels. Global oil, gas, and coal production is predicted to irreversibly decline in the next 10 to 20 years, and severe climate changes are already taking effect around the world."[11]

We can look to the sacred texts of many faiths where we will find sources to inspire us to work for a sustainable planet—a planet that sustains a healthy life for all that dwells therein. Examples from those sacred texts and some interpretations of them are included throughout the book. We begin with four of them.

Ruah Swennerfelt
March 2016

PRAYERS AND POEMS FOR EARTH FROM FOUR TRADITIONS

A Prayer For Our Earth

All-powerful God, you are present in the whole universe

And in the smallest of your creatures.

You embrace with your tenderness all that exists.

Pour out upon us the power of your love,

that we may protect life and beauty.

Fill us with peace, that we may live

as brothers and sister, harming no one.

O God of the poor,

help us to rescue the abandoned and forgotten of this earth,

So precious in your eyes.

Bring healing to our lives,

that we may protect the world and not prey on it,

that we may sow beauty, not pollution and destruction.

Touch the hearts

of those who look only for gain

at the expense of the poor and the earth.

Teach us to discover the worth of each thing,

to be filled with awe and contemplation,

to recognize that we are profoundly united

with every creature

As we journey toward your infinite light,

we thank you for being with us each day.

Encourage us, we pray, in our struggle

for justice, love and peace.

—Pope Francis, Encyclical Letter 2015 [12]

Rededication
A Poem for Tu B'Shevat

Around the midpoint of the globe,
banana palms rustle in the humid air,
while further north (or south) the gnarled branches of live oak
bend low across the centuries. Sugar maples,
linden trees stand stately, stretching skyward.
across the tundra, dwarf birch hunker down.
Without the olive tree, the ner tamid which burned
once in Jerusalem, reminder of God's light,
could not be lit. Without the wild fig and plum
what sweetness would our forebears not have known?
Even in war, the Torah says, fruit trees are sacred:
our battles are not theirs to fight, our job
protection, never sword or flame. Do the trees know
they live enmeshed with us, the air we breathe
enriched as they breath out? Do redwoods mourn
the bite of angry saws when human greed
causes us to forget the earth's not ours to keep?
The full moon shines and paints its liquid silver
on every leaf and branch. And we, who know
that winter's fallow time — even when bitter cold —
conceals the rise of sap, upsurge of energy?
Let us rededicate ourselves. The trees await
The work we need to do. The temple of the earth
besmirched by human hands provides our task, to clean
and set to rights each holy grove. And then
each elm and almond, date, magnolia, laurel tree —
each curry, camphor, willow, oil palm — will praise
the One with every shiver of their branches
as we aspire to offer praise with every breath.

—Rabbi Rachel Barenblat[13]

Declaration of the Four Sacred Things

The earth is a living, conscious being. In company with cultures of many different times and places, we name these things as sacred: air, fire, water, and earth.

Whether we see them as the breath, energy, blood, and body of the Mother, or as the blessed gifts of a Creator, or as symbols of the inter-connected systems that sustain life, we know that nothing can live without them.

To call these things sacred is to say that they have a value beyond their usefulness for human ends, that they themselves become the standards by which our acts, our economics, our laws, and our purposes must be judged. No one has the right to appropriate them or profit from them at the expense of others. Any government that fails to protect them forfeits its legitimacy.

All people, all living beings, are part of the earth life, and so are sacred. No one of us stands higher or lower than any other. Only justice can assure balance; only ecological balance can sustain freedom. Only in freedom can that fifth sacred thing we call spirit flourish in its full diversity.

To honor the sacred is to create conditions in which nourishment, sustenance, habitat, knowledge, freedom, and beauty can thrive. To honor the sacred is to make love possible.

To this we dedicate our curiosity, our will, our courage, our silences, and our voices. To this we dedicate our lives.

—Starhawk, *The Fifth Sacred Thing*[14]

Through the silence of nature,

I attain Thy divine peace.

O sublime nature,

in thy stillness let my heart rest.

Thou art patiently awaiting the moment

to manifest through the silence of sublime nature.

O nature sublime, speak to me through silence,

for I am awaiting in silence like you the call of God.

O nature sublime,

through thy silence I hear Thy cry.

My heart is tuned to the quietness,

that the stillness of nature inspires.

—Hazrat Inayat Khan[15]

CHAPTER 1
BEING FAITHFUL IN A CHANGING WORLD

God is in the water of the lake; he is also in the cracked bed of the lake, when the lake has dried up. God is in the abundant harvest; he is also in the famine that occurs when the harvest fails. God is in the lightning; he is also in the darkness, when the lightning has faded.... Brothers and sisters, you pile up stones to make shrines, imagining that God will make himself present there. Then you are surprised when these shrines do not ease your cares and worries.
  —*366 Readings From Islam,* translated by Robert Van der Weyer[16]

Although we are told that God/Spirit dwells in everything, it is our faith that assures us this is true. As people of faith we seek ways to be faithful to our beliefs. And if we search our own sacred texts, we can find instructions on caring for all that lives.

Being faithful is not about success; it's not about knowing the only right way to solve the problems we face. It's about love. It's about love of ourselves, of our fellow human beings, of all living creatures on Earth. It's about loving as sacred the ground on which we walk. Finding ways to connect and act on our love is the path of the Transition Movement.

There are many people today who question whether climate change and the economic crisis are even real, let alone problems. Among them are many religious people, a segment of whom are uncritical of the *status quo,* anti-science, climate change deniers, or are just too distracted by the corporate-dominated mass media and our consumerist culture. Even among those who no longer deny or dismiss these dangerous global realities, there are still many significant differences.

Some concerned people, for example, see the depth of the modern world's dependence on fossil fuels — as well as the likely supply and demand trends of the future — and then forecast a massive and inevitable global economic depression, and even the collapse of global civilization. Some in this group see the likelihood of a significant die-off of the human population and a chilling "Mad Max" future of small competitive bands fighting each other for scarce resources in an increasingly inhospitable climate. While not impossible as a future outcome, embracing this fatalistic and hopeless outlook is not the Transition vision.

Other people see many of the same threats but think it is still possible to sustain business as usual, at least for the globally privileged and at least for a century or two. These people tend to support high-tech "solutions," such as geo-engineering to deal with climate change. They may respond to projected energy shortages by supporting global resource wars, geopolitical manipulation, intensified global inequality, and undertaking ever more extreme approaches to energy extraction, such as deep-sea oil drilling, tar sands extraction, natural gas hydro-fracturing ("fracking"), and the rapid expansion of uranium mining and nuclear power. This embrace of moral callousness and reckless pursuit of economic growth and political power is also not the Transition vision.

A third group of concerned people envision a more peaceful, equitable, and environmentally friendly future where, as a society, we are able to develop ample safe and renewable energy substitutes for fossil fuels, become more energy efficient, and promote green jobs and poverty-reduction without disrupting global economic growth or dramatically changing the basic contours of our modern way of life. The talk here is of ecological modernization of industry and creating a Green New Deal that reforms key elements of our high energy, corporate-dominated, global economy to promote greater shared prosperity, sustainability, and community well-being. This comes much closer to the Transition vision, but there are still some important differences to consider.

Climate change creates pain, suffering, and violence. Unless we change how we use energy, how we use the land, how we grow our crops, how we treat other animals, and how we use natural resources, we will only further this pain, suffering, and violence. There is something new and unprecedented about our situation today. Our current challenges, for all their similarities with the past, now play out on a much larger, global scale and unfold at a much faster pace than were usually faced by our ancestors. These scale and pace issues are important. There is now a very credible argument to be made that humanity's future might well include a worst-case scenario of global civilizational collapse, massive die-off, and unprecedented worldwide ecological destruction.

As sustainability activist Paul Hawken puts it bluntly, "If you look at the science that describes what is happening on earth today and aren't pessimistic, you don't have the correct data."

Still, for all the prophetic truth in Hawken's claim, we can substitute his word "pessimistic" with the words "deeply concerned." Why? Like our ancestors, we are also called by God to a more loving and faithful way of life where we work to heal and repair the world by building up what Martin Luther King called "the Beloved Community." For all of humanity's obvious pulls towards sinfulness, domination, and subservience, many people throughout history have repeatedly shown the miraculous capacity, with the aid of divine grace and guidance, to be faithful and work together to make a way out of no way. As the Hebrew scriptures say, we are "made in the image of God," and we clearly have the capacity for learning, for love, for cooperation, for forgiveness, for innovation, and for creation. This opens up the possibility for more promising outcomes, even as we face incredibly challenging times now and into the future.

The Miracle of Human Faithfulness

The sacred scriptures of many faith traditions emphasize the importance of seeing and interpreting the signs of times. In the Quran, for example, there is the wonderful concept of *ayat*, which means the signs that God is active in the world. Seeing *ayat* is a core part of Muslim spirituality. Most followers of the Prophet Mohammad, for example, believe that there are clear signs of God in the 6,236 verses of the Quran, but also in the natural world of God's Creation and in the miracles of human faithfulness.

There is a first step each of us needs to take—we need to find our connection to Earth. We need to feel that connection which will motivate us to stand up and work for her survival. And, as Rabbi Andrea Cohen-Kiener in her book, *Claiming Earth as Common Ground*, claims:

> "We may even be reading our texts through our modern eyes, yet very few of us have "green" eyes. Ironically, the first steps out of base camp usually result in a deep reclamation of the dark-green roots of our very own tradition."[17]

So, we need to feel rooted to Earth and then see with "green" eyes. All will be revealed and we won't be able to sit down and ignore the tragedy that surrounds us.

Paul Hawken's book, *Blessed Unrest*, demonstrates that for all the negative global trends that cannot be wished away, there is also an unnamed "movement of movements" emerging across the globe, in which millions of people are working together in their various communities "to restore some semblance of grace, justice, and beauty to this world. ...If you meet the people in this unnamed movement and aren't optimistic, you haven't got a heart."[18]

Hawken first began to "see" this movement of movements when he was traveling around the world giving hundreds of talks on the topics of social justice and sustainability. While on this global speaking tour, Hawken began to notice an almost invariable pattern. After his talks, several people in the audience came up to thank him, and shared stories about their own efforts to, as he put it, "restore, redress, reform, rebuild, recover, reimagine, and reconsider" their communities and world around them. According to Hawken, this happened so many times that "it slowly grew into a hunch that something larger was afoot," perhaps even "a significant social movement that was eluding the radar of mainstream culture."

Hawken then started researching the grassroots social change groups he was hearing about. Over time, he identified more than a million civic organizations around the globe "working on the salient issues of our day: climate change, poverty, deforestation, peace, water, hunger, conservation, and human rights." He also came to the conclusion that even though it rarely shows up on corporate news broadcasts, "this is the largest social movement in all of human history."

While Hawken notes that this emerging movement of movements includes many people who are secular in their outlook, he also documents that many people of faith have become very involved in this work, and often have taken on leadership roles. These spiritual activists get involved to put their faith into action. They have come to believe, just as the Rev. Martin Luther King Jr. did, that "human progress never rolls in on the wheels of inevitability," but always "comes through the tireless efforts and the persistent work of dedicated individuals who are willing to be co-workers with God."[19]

Hawken also believes that at the very heart and soul of this movement of movements are humanity's deepest spiritual insights and aspirations.[18]

One of the most powerful signs among Quakers is the Kabarak Call to Peace and Eco-Justice, a prophetic statement of Quaker faith and practice that was written and sent to Friends everywhere by attenders of the Sixth World Conference of the Religious Society of Friends in 2012. This world conference took place at Kabarak University in Kenya and was the largest and most diverse global gathering of Friends in history. It included more than 850 participants who came from Africa, Asia, the Middle East, Latin America, Europe, and North America. The goal was to listen carefully to the still, small voice of God, as well as to each other. The question was, "What is God calling us to do and be now?"

The resulting revelation was powerful. Sounding like the prophet Hosea, these Quakers from all around the world blasted through their comforting denial about the state of our world. In their statement, they affirmed that it is time for all of us to face some hard truths about the extent and impact of organized sin in our world — and our own complicity in it. As they said:

> "We have heard of the disappearing snows of Kilimanjaro and glaciers of Bolivia, from which come life-giving waters. We have heard appeals from peoples of the Arctic, Asia, and Pacific. We have heard of forests cut down, seasons disrupted, wildlife dying, of land hunger in Africa, of new diseases, droughts, floods, fires, famine and desperate migrations — this climatic chaos is now worsening. There are wars and rumors of war, job loss, inequality, and violence. We fear our neighbors. We waste our children's heritage. All of these are driven by our dominant economic systems — by greed not need, by worship of the market, by Mammon and Caesar. Is this how Jesus showed us to live?"[20]

These Friends answered this last question with a resounding "no," and then made an even bolder move. Not content to reject the worldly sins of domination, denial, and distraction, they also rejected the worldly counsel of despair and inaction. Echoing the psalm that says, "Happy are those who do not follow the advice of the wicked… or sit in the seat of scoffers," these Quakers urged Friends everywhere to become ever more faithful and joyful community activists. As the Kabarak statement declares, "We are called to work for the peaceable Kingdom of God on the whole earth, in right sharing with all peoples."[20]

This statement is now reaching Quakers in their local congregations all around the world. For all the momentary antagon-
isms across the lines of theology, class, culture, and nationality, the
Quakers at this conference ultimately came together in love and
approved the Kabarak Call For Peace and Ecojustice in a nearly
unanimous "sense of the Meeting" decision.

One Kabarak conference participant said he wanted Putney
(Vermont) Friends to hear the Kabarak Call read out loud, as if it
were ministry being offered in one of our most open-hearted and
tender Meetings for Worship. He handed a copy to a member of
the congregation and asked this member to stand and read it to
the group. As this member stood and read the Kabarak Call, it was
not long before he was crying and shaking. The tears did not flow
because of the bad news mentioned early on in the Call. His tears
flowed because of the good news of who we could all become with
God's help. Choked up, he read the following calls to his spiritual
community:

- "We are called to see what love can do: to love our neighbor as
  ourselves, to aid the widow and orphan, to comfort the afflicted
  and afflict the comfortable, to appeal to consciences and bind the
  wounds.

- "We are called to teach our children right relationship, to live in
  harmony with each other and all living beings in the earth, waters
  and sky of our Creator, who asks, "Where were you when I laid
  the foundations of the world?" (Job 38:4)

- "We are called to do justice to all and walk humbly with our God,
  to cooperate lovingly with all who share our hopes for the future
  of the earth.

- "We are called to be patterns and examples in a 21st century campaign for peace and ecojustice, as difficult and decisive as the 18th
  and 19th century drive to abolish slavery.

"We dedicate ourselves to let the living waters flow through us—
where we live, regionally, and in wider world fellowship. We dedicate ourselves to building the peace that passeth all understanding,
to the repair of the world, opening our lives to the Light to guide us
in each small step."[20]

When the member of Putney Friends Meeting finished, this
local Quaker community sat in worshipful silence, letting the
words of the Call enter their hearts. The reader was not the only
one crying at this point. The members of Putney Friends Meeting
felt both convicted and uplifted. After a long time of silent prayer,
they began talking quietly together about how they might move

into a more faithful way of living—one that certainly includes engaging in more creative community activism for peace, justice, and sustainability.

This awakening and transformation is not just a Quaker phenomenon. The World Council of Churches (WCC) has also been engaging in an ecumenical process of reflection and renewal. At their 1998 global conference in Harare, Zimbabwe, the WCC's Assembly posed a similar question to its members: "How do we live our faith in the context of globalization?" At the 2006 Assembly in Porto Alegre, Brazil, the WCC then took a step further and launched a worldwide dialog and research project among its member denominations on "the intrinsic links between poverty, wealth, and ecology." Then a series of continental consultations took place in Africa in 2007, Latin America in 2008, Asia and Pacific in 2009, Europe in 2010, and North America in 2011.[21]

The North American conference offered a confession and a call on behalf of North American churches:

> "We love God, all of Creation, and one another, ... [but] we have failed to live out our love. ... We have left undone those things which we ought to have done, and we have done those things which we ought not to have done. ...
>
> "We see a time of new beginnings, of Jubilee, when greenhouse gases in the atmosphere no longer threaten life, when the carbon economy has been transformed, and we no longer mortgage our children's future. We see a time when unsustainable development has been rejected in favour of just, participatory and sustainable communities. We see a time when the Earth has begun its regeneration and like God with Noah, we have covenanted with God and Creation to never destroy it again... We call on churches, interfaith partners, and all people of goodwill to work together to achieve this timeless and compelling vision."[22]

Another promising sign is the number of already committed "interfaith partners" involved in this work. While spiritual activists may sometimes use different words for the Divine, such as YHWH or Allah, most of them are heeding the call to "seek ye first the Kingdom of God."[23]

Paul Anderson, an evangelical theologian, wisely notes that both Jewish and Christian scriptures testify to the good news that "God is at work in the world, wanting to lead, heal, order, and restore all people to places of ultimate wholeness and joy." Anderson also points out that the goal of faithfulness in both traditions, at least at their best, is "to become a useful conduit of God's healing-redeeming work in the world."[24]

Muslim scholar Dr. Ayse Kadayifc argues that this is just as true of Islam at its best.

"The Qur'anic story of Moses and Exodus clearly warns Muslims today against oppression, violence, corruption, and arrogance, reminding them that we all have a Pharaoh within us. Even when faced with injustice and persecution Muslims need to be just, compassionate, and patient. But neither does the Qur'an ask Muslims to stay idle and accept injustice. On the contrary, the Qur'an asks Muslims to work hard and strive to ensure justice for all through active, creative, nonviolent ways that would restore harmony among God's creation."[25]

In addition to all these inspired statements of faith, there are increasing signs of tangible, hands-on religious activism emerging as well. The feature-length documentary, *Renewal*, made by film-makers Marty Ostrow and Terry Kay Rockefeller, presents eight different case studies from around the United States showing how Evangelicals, mainline Protestants, Anglicans, Roman Catholics, Jews, Muslims, and Buddhists are getting together to take action to foster a more just and sustainable world.[26]

Mark Wallace, Professor of Religion at Swarthmore College, recommends this film because, in a "medium that is visually and viscerally immediate, [it tells] stories of everyday prophets, poets, and preachers who are doing their part to green the planet and care for the physical well-being of the communities and congregations they serve." The film is also profoundly interfaith in its orientation. As Wallace notes, it tells stories of faith-based activism that "range from Christian protests against mountaintop-removal coal mining in Appalachia, to Chicago Muslims partnering with rural farmers to produce organic meat products, to Jewish children in Connecticut learning how to practice Earth-based religion founded on the time-honored beliefs of their ancestors."[27]

The stories in the film range beyond the three monotheistic Abrahamic faiths by including a segment on the Green Sangha Buddhist Community in San Francisco. This spiritual community focuses on its contemplative practice of silent, sitting meditation "to overcome frustration and anger," while also leading a targeted corporate campaign to persuade magazines like *National Geographic* and *The New Yorker* to use only post-consumer, recycled paper products. As Wallace explains, the contribution of such socially engaged, spiritually grounded Buddhism is that it helps all of us to see the big picture that, ultimately, "we are not ideological opponents struggling over dwindling resources, but interconnected brothers and sisters on an evolving planet who mutually depend upon one another for life and well-being."[28]

The final segment of the film tells the story of a dynamic national network of religious congregations called "Interfaith Power & Light" (IPL). Long before organizing IPL, founder Sally Bingham was a high school-educated homemaker who was deeply troubled by how too few religious leaders speak up and call people of faith to take collective action in support of social justice and ecological sustainability. To help rectify this situation, Bingham entered college at the age of 45, went on to seminary, and ultimately became an ordained Episcopal priest. At her first parish, she began preaching a prophetic gospel of faith and action, with a special focus on Creation care and climate protection. She also began working with her congregation to see how their church building could become more energy-efficient and also model the transition away from fossil fuels to safe and green energy sources.

Word of Bingham's creative parish work began to spread throughout her denomination, and she was ultimately able to organize a national team to create the Episcopal Power & Light (EPL) network to expand the scale of this kind of work and support the work of many Episcopal congregations, not just one. The accomplishments of this national network began to inspire congregations from other Christian denominations, and even non-Christian congregations, who started to ask about joining the network and taking part in its ministry. Not long after this, Bingham and the other leaders of EPL realized their faith-based environmental network was becoming more broad-based than they had originally imagined. At this point, they chose to reorganize EPL into a new network called Interfaith Power & Light (IPL). This interfaith environmental network now includes over 18,000 congregations, organized into 40 state chapters. Going even further, IPL also now regularly works in coalition with other faith and secular groups to achieve its goals and build an even more powerful environmental movement.[29]

Vermont Interfaith Power & Light began exploration in 2002 and was officially formed in 2004. The network of members is growing and now includes about 80 congregations, representing Buddhists, Muslims, Jews, Unitarians, and Christians. Their work includes encouraging and supporting congregations to insulate their buildings, upgrade methods of heating and cooling, and produce renewable energy. Although these efforts save the congregations money, most important is their effort to help people of faith see that the concern for Earth is a spiritual concern, motivating them to make changes that are heartfelt.

Learning of the work of faith communities is inspiring. But how do we find a platform that will bring all those communities together with the secular community? We can't contine to try to stop the tide of change that is destroying the livability of our planet without a massive cultural change and that has to happen with the joint efforts of millions of people. The irony is that it has to happen at the grassroots level and that all those efforts in local communities must somehow be the links to a larger whole. Dorothy Day once said, "We must build the new society in the middle of the old, and as the new society grows, it will displace the old."[30] As we will learn in the next chapter, that was the reason the Transition Movement was started, to provide the platform for building a new society. Through its joy, optimism, and hard work we will displace the current culture that tears down life.

Workshop participants experiment with a new Transition game
at the U.K. Transition Conference at Liverpool Hope University.
(*photo by Ruah Swennerfelt*)

CHAPTER 2

PERMACULTURE AND THE BEGINNINGS OF TRANSITION

What an extraordinary time to be alive this is. The systems that are meant to support and provide for us, and to enable us to flourish and thrive, are failing us spectacularly. This is increasingly self-evident to people, wherever they are within those systems. Yet all over the world, in creative, passionate and brave ways, and motivated by a tangible sense of what's possible, people are coming together and creating something else. Something so much better. —Rob Hopkins[31]

Permaculture

The rich soil from which the Transition movement emerged involves many different, thinkers, activists, and movements across time and place. Many of the people who have become involved with the Transition Movement first were engaged in the practices and principles of permaculture, a system of agricultural and social design principles centered around simulating or directly utilizing the patterns and features observed in natural ecosystems. The term "permaculture" was first coined in 1978 by Australians David Holmgren and Bill Mollison.[32] The word permaculture originally referred to "permanent agriculture," but it was expanded to stand also for "permanent culture."

Three core tenets of permaculture:
1) Care for the earth: Provision for all life systems to continue and multiply. This is the first principle, because without a healthy Earth, humans cannot flourish.

2) Care for the people: Provision for people to access those resources necessary for their existence.

3) Return of surplus: Reinvesting surpluses back into the system to provide for the first two ethics. This includes returning waste back into the system to recycle into usefulness. The third ethic is sometimes referred to as Fair Share, to reflect that each of us should take no more than what we need before we reinvest the surplus. And this is the term used in describing the core tenets of the Transition Movement.[32]

12 permaculture design principles:

1) Observe and interact: By taking time to engage with nature we can design solutions that suit our particular situation.

2) Catch and store energy: By developing systems that collect resources at peak abundance, we can use them in times of need.

3) Obtain a yield: Ensure that you are getting truly useful rewards as part of the work that you are doing.

4) Apply self-regulation and accept feedback: We need to discourage inappropriate activity to ensure that systems can continue to function well.

5) Use and value renewable resources and services: Make the best use of nature's abundance to reduce our consumptive behavior and dependence on non-renewable resources.

6) Produce no waste: By valuing and making use of all the resources that are available to us, nothing goes to waste.

7) Design from patterns to details: By stepping back, we can observe patterns in nature and society. These can form the backbone of our designs, with the details filled in as we go.

8) Integrate rather than segregate: By putting the right things in the right place, relationships develop between those things and they work together to support each other.

9) Use small and slow solutions: Small and slow systems are easier to maintain than big ones, making better use of local resources and producing more sustainable outcomes.

10) Use and value diversity: Diversity reduces vulnerability to a variety of threats and takes advantage of the unique nature of the environment in which it resides.

11) Use edges and value the marginal: The interface between things is where the most interesting events take place. These are often the most valuable, diverse and productive elements in the system.

12) Creatively use and respond to change: We can have a positive impact on inevitable change by carefully observing, and then intervening at the right time.[32]

Although not expressed in those terms, permaculture feels very spiritual. Since permaculture informed Transition, it brought those spiritual aspects to Transition. That's how the "Inner Transition" came to be encouraged. And now we'll see how permaculture has enriched someone's life.

Murad Al Khuffash with the author in his permaculture garden
(*photo by Harvey Lewis*)

A Palestinian Permaculture Experience

Murad Al Khuffash, a Palestinian Muslim, has embraced permaculture for farming his family's ten-generation farm. Since permaculture is the foundation for the growth of the Transition Movement, his experiences are valuable for us to get a personal perspective on its importance.

Murad was born in Marda, and has always been a farmer. The farm Murad had transformed into a permaculture farm was once his father's farm. We began our visit in his home, meeting his wife, Ghada, and their three lovely daughters, Sara, Halla, and Toleen. While sitting there we heard the mosque's very loud call to prayer. I asked Murad why he didn't stop to pray, and he explained that he would do it after we left, but we were his guests and he took that seriously.

Murad's English was excellent, since he had lived in the United States for five years to earn money and eventually to take an extensive permaculture workshop. He worked at The Farm in Summertown, Tennessee, which is also home to the Global Village Project, an international NGO. And now his NGO, Marda Permaculture Farm, is a partner project with The Farm and is recognized as a branch of the Global Village Institute.

Palestine has some problems, and Marda brings some new solutions. The farm is an oasis of green in a dry land, where Palestinians have lived under great hardship. Yet there is a promise of a new future. "We believe that permaculture is a key ingredient in the future, not only for Palestine, but for the Middle East and the world. We're setting out to show how it's done," shared Murad.

The Marda Permaculture Farm, started in 2006, is a working farm and a demonstration site for permaculture principles, techniques and strategies. Permaculture, as we have learned earlier, is an ecological design system that draws heavily on indigenous and local wisdom as well as cutting-edge science, to help individuals and communities maximize local resources toward sustainable production, generation and recycling of food, water, energy, housing and other resources.

The project seeks to promote ecological, cultural and economic resilience in the region by developing a small-scale permaculture site to serve as a model and teaching center for local farmers and international permaculture students. Farm staff will also facilitate permaculture design courses in diverse communities across Palestine.

Murad's farm is about two-and-a-half dunams, which is six-tenths of an acre or one-quarter of a hectare. It is amazing how much is being grown in such a small area. Right away you notice the lushness and organic feel of the place and see the prominent and very large greenhouse. Inside the greenhouse tomatoes, cucumbers, zucchini, beans, companion flowers, and more were growing in abundance. Drip irrigation is used so that the small amount of water that is available is used directly on the roots.

For his irrigation, Murad is harvesting rainwater through channels that are used in the town to keep the streets and yards dry, by just directing it to his and other farms. He is teaching others how to use it. At his home he is using the graywater from his washing machine to water the plants in his garden. He has a "no-till" garden, and in among the huge variety of fruit and nut trees and vegetables are lovely places to sit. Many abandoned tires have been used for walls and dividers, and in some cases for planters. The whole small farm is so vibrant and productive—a perfect permaculture garden. We sat in the shade of an olive tree to conduct the interview.

Murad said that he is doing this work because he likes to plant seeds, and watch things grow. He likes to eat healthy food and provide it for others in his village. He also wants to build the movement to help local farmers see how productive permaculture farming is. He has a vision of building a house on the site, creating electricity from solar panels, and becoming self-sufficient. He then wants the farmers in the village, after adopting permaculture ethics, to sell to outside markets, marketing the organic vegetables and fruits, bringing some economic security to an economically depressed area. His vision includes diversity of crops so that a farmer isn't wiped out from one crop failure. Also he plants crops that mature throughout the year, helping to bring income on a more regular schedule. He does believe that his project will help create global health through teaching internationals who come to learn permaculture.

Because his family has been farming in Marda for so many generations, Murad is known and respected in town and has more of an opportunity to influence his neighbors than outside NGOs bringing the message. We returned to his home to a splendid lunch with his family. Murad has continued to host permaculture courses on his farm, one of which was recently led by Starhawk. He continues to encourage his friends and neighbors to adopt permaculture as a way of life in Marda. Because he is passionate about building resilience in his town, and is laying the framework for a stronger, sharing community, maybe next will come a Transition Town Marda!

Murad was able to adapt what he learned from the permaculture courses to farming in a country where he and his neighbors are denied the right to water. Permaculture provides a foundation, not a prescriptive state of rules that one must follow. It encourages creativity and ingenuity because it has to be adapted to the community in which it rises. That is the big secret to its success, as we shall see.

Rob Hopkins's Journey
from Permaculture to Transition

The early roots of the Transition Movement involve a permaculture teacher and his students, who engaged in lively discussion, reflection, and experimentation together in Kinsale, Ireland.

Rob Hopkins moved to Ireland in the late 1990s with a strong interest in setting up a small, countercultural, eco-village in the Irish countryside and teaching people the principles and practices of permaculture. He was a professor at Kinsale College of Further Education in Kinsale, Ireland, while living in a nearby intentional community. He was also a permaculture designer.

Rob Hopkins
(photo by Jim Wileman)

Upon arriving in Ireland, Rob soon had the opportunity to teach and organize permaculture classes. Over the next few years, the course topics included organic agriculture and gardening, natural building, whole foods nutrition, field ecology, ecological design, and woodlot management, as well as modules in small business management, conflict resolution, and community leadership skills. This work eventually expanded into a popular, two-year Permaculture Certificate Program in Practical Sustainability—the first such program in the world.

It was in the midst of this work that Rob and his students started consciously examining the strengths and the weaknesses of the permaculture movement in light of the intensifying global ecological crisis. They worked to deepen their analysis, vision, and strategy in order to become more effective in social change work.

For Rob and his students, one of the more influential articles they discussed was "A Second Challenge to the Movement," a piece written by Eric Stewart for the *Permaculture Activist*. What rang most true for them was the notion that, "Permaculture as it stands on the verge of its 'call to power,' appears to have a built-in flaw." According to Rob, the most challenging passages in Stewart's article were:

"It seems to me that permaculture houses two virtually polar impulses; one involves removal from the larger society; the other involves working for the transformation of society. While the case can be made that removal from the larger society represents action that is transformative of society, I believe that there is an imbalance with the cultural manifestation of permaculture that has favored isolation over interaction. The cultural shift we need depends on increasing interaction to increase the availability of the resources permaculture offers. Are we thinking big enough? Are we in danger of becoming irrelevant just at the time when permaculture is at its most relevant? We need to ramp our game up, so how might we do that?"[33]

While reflecting on their own experience in Kinsale and articles like this, Rob and his students chose not to abandon their roots in permaculture, but instead started pushing the idea that permaculture should become a much more inclusive, larger-scale, approach to community organizing and design. Indeed, Rob and many of his students concluded that there was a real need for the permaculture movement to rise to the challenge of ending its backwoods, counter-culture distance from where most people live, work, and play, and help instead to foster "a massive-scale social transformation."

"What my students and I increasingly wanted to do was issue a call to the bodgers and chairmakers in the woods, the market gardeners and orchardists up misty rural lanes, the small-scale wind installers on the windswept highlands, to bring all the wonderful skills they have accumulated, the insights they have obtained through years of practice and contemplation, back to where the mass of the population is starting to realize things are not right."

The urgency of this goal was only heightened by the emerging scientific consensus on global warming and, perhaps even more important, by what Rob and his students began to learn about the likely social and economic impacts of "peak oil."

"Prior to September 2004 I had never heard of the concept of peak oil. On the first day of term, the students were shown a new film called *The End of Suburbia*, and then, later that day, Dr. Colin Campbell of the Association for the Study of Peak Oil gave a talk to the students. The reaction was intense. This educational 'double whammy' was powerful and greatly focused the mind, and came as quite a shock to everyone — myself included.

"Once the mental dust had settled, the concept emerged of a project for the second-year permaculture students. On the assumption that Campbell's forecasts would be proved true, they set out to explore how the town of Kinsale might successfully make the transition to a lower energy future."

This collaborative research project finally resulted in the drafting and publication of *Kinsale 2021: An Energy Descent Action Plan*. Rob and the students hoped to demonstrate to local people that "life with less oil could, if properly planned for and designed, be far preferable to the present." The report seemed to resonate with many of the citizens of the village of Kinsale, and the plan was eventually adopted by Kinsale's Town Council.

In 2005, Kinsale College hosted a "Fueling the Future" conference, with such notable speakers as Richard Heinberg (author, educator, and speaker on peak oil), David Holmgren (co-originator of the permaculture concept), and Eamoun Ryan (who later was Ireland's Minister for Energy for four years and represented the Green Party). This conference was a great success, and in early 2006 the Kinsale Town Council gave €5,000 as support for Kinsale's Energy Descent Plan (later Kinsale Transition Town). Rob's work with his students to develop that Energy Descent Plan for Kinsale helped him find a solution.

After much consideration, Rob and his family decided they wanted to return to England. So Rob moved to Totnes to see whether he could scale up his embryonic ideas of a new way of life. Two people involved in peak oil came to give talks, author Richard Heinberg and the late David Flemming, one of England's peak oil whistle blowers. Along with other friends and neighbors, Rob started reflecting on the Kinsale experience in preparation for their own community-organizing efforts in Totnes.

Some of the insights that he and the others developed together through their discussions included:

- Being more community-based rather than just campus-based,

- Developing a well-organized and ongoing steering group,

- Engaging in much more awareness-raising activities with all sectors of the community,

- Seeking out much more comment and input from community members on future directions for their community,

- Preparing the ground for future energy descent planning involving the city government, and

- Beginning a preparation period for the energy descent planning that involved a wide variety of hands-on organizing projects that helped to unleash the creativity of the local community and build a stronger base for Transition thinking and culture.

There is little doubt that the emerging Transition Movement grows out of a rich cultural soil, built up over centuries. The "earthworms" of this historic soil-building process are very diverse, but they certainly include the insights and practices of many spiritually grounded thinkers, activists, and social entrepreneurs. In his book, *The Transition Companion*, Rob Hopkins lists a number of "trailblazers and assorted sources of inspiration" for the Transition Movement in just the last 60 years or so. On his list are several religious and spiritual practitioners, including Martin Luther King Jr., Rosa Parks, E.F. Schumacher, Joanna Macy, Bill McKibben, Gary Snyder, Satish Kumar, and Vandana Shiva. He has noted that traditional faith-based communities have crafted local ways of life based on very different assumptions than those embodied in modern neoliberal, corporate capitalist societies. These have served as important sources of inspiration for the Transition Movement.

"In 1990 I visited the Hunza Valley in northern Pakistan and got my first tantalizing glimpses of a society that lived within its limits and had evolved a sophisticated yet simple way of doing so. This was before I knew anything about permaculture, or the concept of resilience, or even a great deal about food, farming or the environment. Yet, in the Hunza Valley's network of traditional Muslim farming villages and towns, I found the most beautiful, tranquil, happy, and abundant place I have ever visited before or since.

"This realization came as somewhat of a shock to me because I had grown up in England when the fossil fuel party was in full swing, in a culture ceaselessly trying to erase all traces of resilience and rubbishing the very idea at every opportunity, portraying country people as stupid, and growth and 'progress' as inevitable. We have to be careful not to romanticize or idealize this relatively remote region of Pakistan by ignoring its challenges or problems. But if at that time the Hunza would have been cut off from the world and the global economy's highways of trucks packed with goods, it would have managed fine. If there were a global economic downturn, or even a collapse, it would have had little impact on the Hunza Valley. The people were resilient, happy, and healthy, and had a strong sense of community.

"In this remote valley I felt a yearning for something I couldn't quite put my finger on but which I now see as being resilient: a culture based on its ability to function indefinitely, to live within its limits, and to thrive for having done so.

"In 1990 I participated in a Buddhist religious community. I lived in a Tibetan Buddhist community in Italy, where I grew fascinated by the depth of wisdom and insight in the tradition. In this spiritual community, I was deeply moved by the practice of daily meditation and the community's focus on compassion, letting go of greed and egotism, cultivating right relationship with all sentient beings, and embracing the value of both inner and outer transformation through 'skillful means.'

"I became increasingly aware of just how easy it is to miss the point of such spiritual wisdom, especially while living in a highly individualistic, often self-serving, consumerist culture. I grew weary of the disconnection between theory and practice among some of the Western practitioners of Buddhism, especially when it came to environmental issues.

"There we were discussing mindfulness practice while at the same time buying all our food from the supermarket and filling the dustbins with compostable waste. This situation did not sit well with me. I was feeling a growing call inside myself to find positive, practical, and loving ways to help foster 'an extraordinary renaissance — economic, cultural, and spiritual' throughout the industrialized world.

"It was around this time that I came across an article that Ken Jones had written on socially engaged Buddhism and 'walking the talk' with regard to environmental issues. It had a profound effect on me, putting clearly what I had been thinking but had not quite managed to articulate yet. ...[Jones' spiritually-grounded] insights on activism and social change are of great relevance to those of us designing methods for engaging communities in energy descent work."

Rob holds an M.Sc. in Social Research and had recently completed a Ph.D. at the University of Plymouth, with a dissertation entitled "Localisation and Resilience at the Local Level: the Case of Transition Town Totnes." What drew Rob to his work on Transition and resilience?

"I think the spark was a fairly long night of the soul after seeing the video, *The End of Suburbia* and Colin Campbell coming into my class of students in Kinsale and talking about peak oil. I had never ever thought about it before. I had been involved in environmental things for years and years and I had never even clocked it as an issue and it came so out of nowhere.

"Until then I had been following the traditional permaculture path of building my own house, growing my own food, planting my forest garden, gathering my water, and generating my own energy.

"The concept of 'peak oil' came out of the blue and tipped everything on its head. Where I lived I was dependent on my car to make connections with my friends. I was struggling with this dilemma when, a month later, the house I was building burned down. With everything thrown up in the air, I looked around for people focused on the peak oil issue. Other than the Post Carbon Institute and some re-localization folks, not many had it on their radar. I read David Holmgren's book, *Permaculture: Principles and Pathways Beyond Sustainability*, with a small group of people and was excited by it. But there weren't any guidelines about how we might restructure our lives to survive in a post-oil society."

Naresh Giangrande

Serendipitously, Rob Hopkins met Naresh Giangrande in a pub around 2005. Three years before, Naresh had received an e-mail from a friend about how rapidly Earth's climate was changing, and it woke him up to the immediacy of the problem, recognizing that it was something his generation had to deal with. After a lot of research, he also learned about peak oil and began giving talks wherever he could.

While visiting Totnes, Naresh found a kindred spirit in Rob Hopkins. In particular, Rob's practice of permaculture seemed to offer a new way of looking at and dealing with peak oil and climate change and other major systemic problems. The two decided to collaborate, and the Transition Movement was born. Rob wrote the book and Naresh created the trainings. Naresh asks himself from time to time whether there is any other urgent task that might take him away from Transition work, and the answer is always, "No," because Transition is such a positive, nurturing, hopeful process. The viral way it is spreading to so many people and places gives him hope. At the All-France Transition Conference in 2011, Naresh shared some of his thoughts about Transition.

Naresh Giangrande
(*photo by Ruah Swennerfelt*)

"The challenge for our times is how to create the Transition. My vision includes a re-localized economy and living more simply with reduced mobility. But what excites me is how to create system change, how to move from where we are to where we need to get. The vision needs to be informed by hard science as well as our feelings and our intuitions. A hundred years ago in Totnes we used to create the cake and import the icing. Today we import the cake and create only the icing. We need to turn that back around. Totnes is a town with lots of agricultural land around, and so the transition is really possible there.

"There is a concern by many that small town life will be boring if we don't have the level of external entertainment to rely on. How can we assure people that life can be rich and full through relationships instead of relying on what we now consider entertainment?

"I see the deep cynicism in the young people I meet who no longer believe that the current system will give them what they need. I believe that we are in the meltdown phase and that an Inner Transition is an essential part of the Transition Movement. As I do this work and change inside, I see that there are times when I go into a 'liquid state,' and that's the state where I think we are in—entering this liquid state and people are going in many directions, eco-villages, Transition work, etc. and this multi-directional quest for a changing world gives me hope."

At the end of a Transition Training, Naresh doesn't tell the participants to now go out and do Transition work; he instead says "Don't go out and create a Transition Town—go out and do something different. We need diversity, and we'll be the geese honking you on your way.'"

Co-founded by Rob Hopkins and Naresh Giangrande, Transition Totnes was kicked off and went viral!

Transition Network Created

Another incredible moment was when Ben Brangwyn, attending an early Transition conference, said, "You need a network to support this work, and I'm willing to give it a year of my time to make it happen." And so the Transition Network came about because of the dedication and creativity of Ben Brangwyn and a number of other people, too many to name here.

Rob Hopkins' Vision of the future

"Like an overlay of many different things I have already seen, the future is not something just created in the mind. It is very tangible and real, but it would be inherently local, with much less intrusive advertising to encourage purchasing things we don't need. Food would be grown everywhere, in the cities on small bits of ground and rooftops. One day growing food would be seen as a really cool, hip occupation. Being a young entrepreneurial market gardener is going to be like what Bob Dylan was in 1963.

"Buildings would be constructed of recycled materials and hand-crafted lovingly and with pride. Buildings would be made for the community and by the community with skilled craftspeople, such as was done in centuries past. The great cathedrals of Europe took up to 120 years to build, and many people worked faithfully on these projects knowing they would never live to see them completed! Local currencies and local banks supported that work.

"This future place is a really vibrant and really delicious place to wake up and be part of, a really thrilling place. It is all do-able! What Transition does is help people think about scaling up what they are doing. For example, the straw-bale house builder might have a goal of building no more than a few a year, but Transition can provide the incentive, the vision, and the creativity for scaling this up to build houses for many people. This is the cutting edge of the Transition movement today.

"Transition is growing up. It is about becoming relevant to the community, creating livelihoods and a sound economic system for the post-oil world. In one of the workshops someone asked, 'what would it look like if you organized the awareness raising stage of your Transition Initiative as a social enterprise?' Wow!

"Resilience is something that needs to happen everywhere, not just here in the developed world. We've creamed the fat off the developing world for the last 400 years, and the idea that we would put up the fence and say 'we'll not sort this out for ourselves' is irresponsible. We need to have two processes that run in parallel — re-localization here, understanding that total re-localization is impossible, but maybe working toward an 80-percent/20-percent mix of local and imported goods. There's the process of contraction and convergence, with the developed world scaling down and the developing world scaling up. Helping to create food security in the developing world is really necessary.

"Over the last four years, people have asked what Transition would be like in the developing world. I responded, 'I have no idea!' I hope they will sort it out for themselves. I have been very impressed with the work that Transition is doing in Brazil.

"The people in each Initiative have to figure out what works for them. One London Transition group came to ask how Transition would work in their economically challenged area and again received the reply, 'I don't have any idea, go sort it out for yourselves.' Now that group has done amazing things. Having several people in the group attend the Transition training was helpful, but each location has its own challenges, culture, and environment. There isn't one blueprint that fits all.

"In *The Transition Companion* there is a quote off the sleeve notes of the Velvet Underground 1969 Live album, 'I wish it was a hundred years from now, I can't stand the suspense.' The beauty of Transition is that you do see the unfolding successes and you start to get a taste of it. In Totnes, in the five years since we started, I can now walk down the street and see 200 nut trees we planted. We had our first harvest of almond trees in the park, there's food being grown where there was none before, there are 150 solar systems that weren't there before.... It gives you a taste of what's possible and drives you on to the next bit.

Heart and Soul of Transition

"It wasn't very long into the evolution of Transition in Totnes, in 2006, that Hilary Prentice and Sophy Banks came round to my house to discuss the seeds of what would eventually become known as 'Inner Transition', or the 'Heart and Soul' of Transition. I remember little about the hour that we passed in my lounge, but I do remember that something felt instinctively right. Their argument was that any successful Transition process needed to be as much about the inner life of the people and groups making it happen, with attention paid to group health, dynamics and resilience, as it needed to be about solar panels, carrots, and Energy Descent Plans. It made a lot of sense. And it still makes a lot of sense today: which is why so many people want to hear more about it.

"Now the concept of Inner Transition runs through Transition like a golden thread, although admittedly more in some places than others. Transition has always stood on the shoulders of many great movements that came before it, and has tried to learn, where possible, from their experience. Burnout and conflict have long been the Achilles Heel of bottom-up activism."

Steve Chase's Journey to Transition

Steve Chase is a member of Putney Friends Meeting in Vermont, a co-founder of Transition Keene Advocates, and the Director of Pendle Hill, a Quaker adult education center. He has been active in the Transition national training network and has

written numerous articles on faith, social activism, environmental justice, sustainability, and the Transition Movment. He tells the story of his journey to the Transition Movement.

"On February 22, 2010, the national non-profit organization Transition US sent out a press release about myself, and a handful of my friends and neighbors in Keene, New Hampshire. Inspired by the international Transition movement and the writings of Rob Hopkins, the seven of us had recently formed Transition Keene Advocates and had successfully applied to be recognized as an official Transition Initiative. This small nugget of news was the gist of the Transition US press release.

Steve Chase
(photo by John Meyer)

According to the release, Transition Keene was 'the 56th official Transition Initiative in the United States and the first official Transition Initiative in New Hampshire.' I smiled when I read the release and said to myself, 'OK, it's official—I'm a local Transition organizer.'"

This turn of events was not much of a surprise to either Steve's family or long-time friends. Becoming a local Transition organizer is remarkably consistent with his activist evolution and spiritual journey over the years. In the mid-1970s he had helped to organize a series of weekly study circles for environmental, peace, and social justice activists in Minneapolis and Saint Paul.

"Our aim was to help each other see beyond the next demonstration, the next hot-button issue, or even the next volunteer shift at the food coop or community garden. Several of us sensed that we needed to go beyond our urgent, but largely unreflective activism. We wanted to create a more thoughtful politics than our heart-felt, but somewhat knee-jerk responses to date. The assembled participants in this series of study circles had decided to work together in order to construct a deeper, more mature analysis, vision, and strategy to guide our activist work in an emerging age of global ecological crisis.

"I loved our living room gatherings in the Twin Cities. Each week, after a potluck supper, we would settle in for two and a half hours of reports and discussions based on our readings and our experiences. The learning process was participatory and lively—consciously rooted in the popular education theories of Paulo Freire and Myles Horton. Topics of the study circles included the environmental crisis, ecological limits to growth, North-South relations, U.S. social-justice issues, militarism, alternative social and economic visions, Gandhian nonviolence, and other organizing strategies. The curriculum for these 'Macro-Analysis Seminars' was developed as a program of activist self-study designed by a Philadelphia group that was part of a national activist network called the Movement for a New Society."

The frame that they were developing in those study groups was, in many ways, similar to the emerging Transition Model of today, and what Sociologist Bob Edwards called "collective action frames."

"Collective action frames are narrative maps guiding movements toward their goals. Frames include interpretations of the injustice or immorality of specific social conditions, an attribution of blame for them, some kind of action agenda for solving them, and a motivation for taking that action. They are interpretative symbolic schemes socially constructed by movements to orient their actions in an ever-shifting political, social, and cultural context. Because the social and political landscape is dynamic and fluid, movement frames evolve over time as groups revise them in light of changing circumstances and accumulating experience."[34]

Steve especially remembers reading and discussing Bill Moyers's 1972 groundbreaking essay, *De-Developing the United States Through Nonviolence*. Moyers explained how modern industrialized societies would at some point need to make a significant break from the dominant development model of ever-escalating economic growth and ever-expanding energy use and pollution. In light of new research, such as the groundbreaking *Limits to Growth* report put together by a team of MIT scientists, Moyers argued that there is increasing evidence that "there are not enough resources (including minerals, fossil fuels, water), and the environment's pollution-absorption capacity is not great enough" to sustain the dominant pattern of industrial development for too many more decades.[35]

Anticipating the problems of peak oil, climate change, and the unsustainability and injustice of the global economy, which are all highlighted by the Transition Movement today, Moyers argued that "complete world development" along the lines of the dominant industrial growth model is impossible. He then concluded that "over-developed" industrial nations like the United States will have to choose between intensifying their war against the poor and the planet, while still risking future decline or collapse, or "de-developing" themselves and finding ways to transition to a more just, sustainable, and fulfilling way of life. As Moyers noted in the piece, "In this long-range vision of a more egalitarian world in which the industrialized nations are de-developed, the standards of happiness would be based more on human relationships and individual actualization than quantities of material consumption."

Steve remembers that Moyers's unconventional perspective challenged those in the study groups because back then, almost all progressive activists still claimed that we could grow our way out of imperialism, poverty, and war by forever expanding the economic pie available to all people.

"Following Moyers's ecological perspective, however, most of us in the study groups were able to begin moving beyond the dominant pro-growth consensus. Several of us in the Twin Cities, and several others influenced by Moyers's thinking around the country, went on to assist the formation of a regionally-rooted, but nationally-networked movement that waged numerous nonviolent direct action campaigns across the country opposing the proposed construction of 1,000 new nuclear reactors in the United States, which we saw as a dangerous and very flawed attempt to maintain the dominant model of 'business as usual.'

"This particular 'de-development' movement was ultimately successful at capping the number of U.S. nuclear reactors at under 200, which is a significant victory, even though we wished the final number had been zero. At this point in U.S. history, and perhaps given the limits of our overly oppositional organizing model, we were not able to build a strong enough movement to go farther and achieve our long-range vision of a transition to a decentralized, non-nuclear, post-oil economy built on a foundation of extensive energy conservation, an overall reduction in global energy demand, and switching to safe and renewable energy sources produced largely at the local and regional level.

Then by 1980, Moyers with Pamela Haines (from the Movement for a New Society), had written a new piece, "No Nukes is Not Enough," stressing even more urgently that the anti-nuke movement would be wise to reframe itself as a positive, safe-energy movement and "actively advocate alternatives as well."

"We need to be calling for a shift from the traditional hard energy path of massive centralized generating plants using nonrenewable fuels to a new soft-energy path of flexible decentralized generation, based on a diversity of mostly renewable energy sources. ... It is not enough to add [the fossil fuels industry] to nuclear power as another system that must be fought. We need a vision of what we want America's energy future to look like, so that we can develop a strategy for the citizens' movement to get from here to there. Without a vision, we don't know where we are going, we get frustrated and stuck in protest, and don't have a basis for deciding what to do next. It is also important to have some ideas of what the transition period looks like so we can have benchmarks for recognizing our victories along the way."[36]

Now, 35 years later, this unfinished agenda has been strongly taken up again by the international Transition Movement. Today, we can see that these visionary themes are being picked up, updated, and expanded in the Transition Movement's call for re-localization efforts to foster community resilience, promote energy descent planning, and move forward on the redevelopment of sound local economies that are equitable and sustainable. Such a constructive, community-driven program for a more re-localized and sustainable world was certainly raised up for our consideration in Moyers's writings, but even he left it largely undeveloped in light of his more urgent priority of challenging nuclear power plant construction through local nonviolent civil disobedience campaigns. With the Transition Movement, this largely neglected element of Moyers's and Haines's thinking is now being put front and center.

In all his work as an activist and activist educator since the 1980s, Steve has been puzzling over, and experimenting with, how to move toward the long-range, sustainability vision that was first brought to his attention by people like Bill Moyers and Pamela Haines.

"After all these years, one of my core conclusions is that it is no longer sufficient to put all our hopes into a mass revival of using the grass-roots social-action tools of electoral campaigning, voting responsibly, lobbying our elected officials, or putting real 'street heat' under corporate or government officials by participating in nonviolent protests and direct action campaigns. Is this sacrilege?

"Please don't get me wrong. I believe that all of these forms of civic engagement are still important and still needed — and should be engaged in by active citizens everywhere. Yet, like most Transition organizers, I have also come to believe that something else—something very important—needs to be added into the mix of our activism and placed much closer to the center of our work. That something is a networked global movement of community-by-community, grassroots organizing. Such organizing is aimed at creating re-localized, resilient, and sustainable communities through positive, practical, citizen-led projects and alternative institutions—essentially what Gandhi called the 'constructive program,' which he saw as a vital complement to his more well-known nonviolent 'resistance program.'"

Researcher Peter North acknowledges that a growing number of people all around the world have begun organizing along these lines to replace the high-energy, oil-addicted, neoliberal global economy with a diversity of community-driven, post-carbon, low-energy, economic re-localization initiatives.

"Contemporary localization is advocated by Green Parties, advocates of small-is-beautiful alternative production, by participants in local-currency networks, by opponents of supermarkets and other 'big box' large retailers, and by members of localist think tanks such as the New Economics Foundation, the EF Schumacher Society, the Institute for Local Self Reliance, or the International Forum on Globalization. It is now proposed as a solution to Peak Oil and climate change. ... One of the best organized and most promising re-localization efforts around the world is the international Transition Movement.[37]

Other observers agree. Phil England of the *New Internationalist* says, "The Transition movement is the best news there's been for a long time." Patrick Holden, the Director of the British Soil Association, says, "The Transition concept is one of the big ideas of our time. ... What I love about the Transition approach is that it is inspirational, harnessing hope instead of guilt, and optimism instead of fear."[38]

In his Foreword to *The Transition Handbook*, U.S. peak oil expert Richard Heinberg argues that there are thousands of post-oil/relocalization efforts underway in various communities around the world, but "there is something different about the Transition network—a sense of excitement, possibility, and engagement, perhaps powered by their ongoing development of a replicable strategy for harnessing the talents, vision, and goodwill of ordinary people."[39]

In his own research on the various streams of emerging post-oil/relocalization movement, environmental author John Michael Greer agrees with Heinberg that "the most widely known of [these efforts], and the most successful so far, is the Transition Town movement."[40]

For those less familiar with the Transition Movement, Steve offers a quick sketch of the movement and its evolution:

"Local Transition Initiatives start when a small collection of motivated individuals within a community come together with a shared concern: how can our community respond to the challenges and opportunities of peak oil, climate change and the economic crisis?

"This was the big question that brought my friends and neighbors together to form the initial Transition Keene organizing group. Yet, what really excited us was the unusual and positive way that the Transition model seeks to address these issues. The core goals of local Transition movements are to generate hope, unleash the collective creativity of local folks to envision a more resilient and whole community, and then encourage the creation of many local working groups and projects that can accelerate a community's transition to a low-carbon, energy-lean way of life that is also ecologically sustainable, socially just, and spiritually fulfilling."

Often a seed begins to germinate and then dies from lack of water, poor soil, or adverse climate. So goes the lives of many small organizations. The ideas are good, but for whatever reason, the seed of the idea does not take root. Not so in the case of the seed idea of the Transition Movement. Watered by many creative and dedicated people, the seed set roots in fertile soil and began to flourish. In the next chapter we shall read how that flourishing grew tall and spread its branches across the planet.

CHAPTER 3
THE EMERGENCE AND GROWTH OF TRANSITION

From now till the point where we don't talk about Transition because it's happened, looking back, we'll see many small communities working well together. Bicycles will be the main sort of transportation. We won't have supermarkets. We'll have a successful system of agriculture that will support the city. It will all be localized. We'll breathe cleaner.[41]

—Penny Skerret, 2011, Transition City Manchester, England, UK

This is typical of the positive thinking of so many people involved in the Transition Movement. Though the world is crumbling around them, they are involved and excited by the prospect of real change. A growing percentage of people around the world, including many people of faith, share the Transition Movement's concerns over the looming threats of climate change, resource limits, and an increasingly dysfunctional global economy, but not the Transition Movement's evolving vision of constructive engagement based on permaculture principles.

People in the Transition Town Movement tend to believe that we will likely need even more fundamental social changes in our politics, economics, and culture if we are to successfully embody the permaculture principles of "Earth Care, People Care, and Fair Share" while we are faced with potentially severe climate disruption and a much smaller usable global energy supply than is currently available.

The key watchwords here are: powering down; re-localizing the economy; shifting from massive levels of "free trade" to modest levels of "fair trade;" adopting permaculture design principles and practices at all levels of the community; re-skilling for greater local self-reliance and home production; enhancing grassroots democracy; encouraging neighborliness and sharing; unleashing community creativity and innovation; strengthening small businesses,

45

nonprofits, cooperatives, and community-owned enterprises; and revitalizing the heart and soul of community life, while embracing simple living and letting go of the culture of conspicuous consumption. These are some of the elements of the Transition vision.

There are also some unique strategies at play too. While acknowledging the value of campaigning for corporate accountability, changes in national public policy, and new international treaties, the fundamental focus of the Transition Movement is sparking thousands, and ultimately millions, of community-led initiatives around the world. These initiatives are developing positive, solutions-oriented, constructive programs for promoting energy descent, economic re-localization, and rebuilding local community resilience. It is widely believed in Transition Town circles that if we wait for our governments, it'll be too little, too late; if we only act as individuals, it'll be too little; but if we act as communities, it might just be enough, just in time.

What if people in towns or sections of cities got together regularly for local foods potlucks, discussions about sharing resources and building resilience, listening to speakers and watching films, making music, and having fun? Can we imagine bringing people together who are from different political viewpoints, different economic conditions, different cultures, different races, different educational backgrounds, and different religious beliefs? How can obstacles to that vision be overcome?

How will we live as we enter the post-carbon world? What if the communities we each call home had seriously prepared for the end of cheap, abundant fossil fuels? What might that look like? The Transition Town Movement encourages people to come together to address these questions and explore how they might be addressed.

Many today say we must put climate change as the number-one priority. But actions like writing letters to governments and corporations, attending protests, and reducing our own carbon footprint—all very important things that help make us feel like we are making a difference—are not enough. To stabilize and revitalize our faltering industrialized civilization and Earth's deteriorating biosystems, we must somehow bring about systemic or structural change. Rising to the challenge to create strong, resilient, and healthy communities where we can work together has to be part of the solution.

The Transition Movement as One Way Forward

The attraction of the Transition movement is that it rests on practical and local initiatives to meet the challenge not only of peak oil, but also of climate change and of the ongoing financial and economic crisis.

—Timothy Gorringe and Rosie Beckham[42]

A community-based, internationally networked movement focused on promoting this vision has been called for by a number of people over the years. For example, resource economist Richard Heinberg describes the kind of movement he thinks we need to develop:

"It should aim to build community resilience, taking account of local vulnerabilities and opportunities. Ideally, this movement should frame its vision of the future in positive, inviting terms. It should aim to build a cooperative spirit among people with differing backgrounds and interests. While this movement should be rooted in local communities, its effectiveness would increase if it were loosely coordinated through national hubs and a global information center. The work of local groups should include the sharing of practical skills such as food production and storage, home insulation, and the development and use of energy conserving technologies. The movement should be non-authoritarian, but should hold efficient meetings, training participants in effective, inclusive decision-making methods."[43]

Happily, as Heinberg reports, we are in luck, because the emerging Transition Town Movement matches this desired prescription in all key respects. As many other scholars, activists, and journalists have noted, the Transition Town Movement is perhaps the fastest growing coordinated effort along these lines. The Movement is probably best described in the three books by Rob Hopkins, a British Buddhist permaculture teacher and one of the Transition Movement's most visible co-founders and leaders.[44]

The original goals of the early Transition organizers were twofold. First, they wanted to foster many citizen-led local projects, workgroups, and businesses to promote community resilience, economic re-localization, and a planned energy descent in their town. Second, they hoped to serve as an inspirational model for how other concerned local citizens could face the threats of climate change, resource depletion, and economic instability with courage, creativity, and a positive vision in their own communities. As we shall see, the early organizers of Transition Town Totnes have been remarkably successful on both counts.

Like the Montgomery Bus Boycott, which sparked the Civil Rights Movement in the United States back in 1955, Transition Totnes has sparked similar local community organizing initiatives elsewhere. As noted by Rob, it did not take long before "other places were getting in touch to ask what we were doing. ...The demand became such that we set up an organization called the Transition Network to more effectively support them." That was in 2008.

One exciting aspect of Transition is the possibility of its working in any language or any country. There's no one right way to do it except with the expectation that the core permaculture values of "Earth Care, People Care, and Fair Share" will prevail—that we will come together with open minds and hearts to learn from each other and share our ideas. It's a place where we each will be respected, listened to, and laughed with. We can bring our values, ideas, hopes, and visions, and see them take shape within our daily lives.

As of the spring of 2016, there were more than 1,200 Transition Initiatives in 50 countries, using 17 languages! These local initiatives are taking root in rural villages, small towns, inner city neighborhoods, streets, suburbs, and even islands in both the global North and the global South. Many Transition organizers also stay connected to each other through regional, national, and international network "hubs," such as the Transition Network, Transition US, and the Middle Atlantic Transition Hub.

These networking groups now offer websites, blogs, webinars, downloadable manuals, listservs, conference calls, organizer trainings, face-to-face conferences, intervisitation, and a few modestly paid staff. One of their most important functions is sharing the growing number of helpful insights, organizing tools, inspirational case studies, and lessons in positive community change and social entrepreneurship being developed within different local initiatives. This work is also aided by Rob's blog, *Transition Culture*, the publication of the online journal, *Transition Voices*, the videos, *In Transition 1.0* and *In Transition 2.0*, and Rob's 2014 book, *21 Stories of Transition*.

Most of the organizers of local Transition Initiatives, and their networking support organizations, are animated by what Rob calls the Transition Movement's "four key assumptions." It is assumed that:

1) life with dramatically lower energy consumption is inevitable and that it's better to plan for it than to be taken by surprise;

2) our settlements and communities presently lack the resilience to enable them to weather the severe energy shocks that will accompany peak oil;

3) we have to act collectively, and we have to act now; and

4) by unleashing the collective genius of those around us to creatively and proactively design our energy descent, we can build ways of living that are more connected, more enriching, and recognize the biological limits of our planet.

Even people who might not agree with all four of these assumptions are often attracted to local Transition Movement organizing. In all his years of promoting the Transition message, Rob says he has yet "to encounter anyone who thinks that stronger local economies, increased local democracy, strengthened local food culture and more local energy production are bad ideas." The organizing approach is collaborative, fun, creative, open-ended, constructive, inclusive, and local—a scale that many people can imagine working at, even if they have lost hope in national politics and political parties.

Transition asks people to imagine where they would like their place or community to be in 5, 10, 20, 50 years' time. It can be challenging to exercise our visionary muscles, but for many people it is also encouraging and even energizing.

The Transition Movement's evolving vision also appears capable of attracting people who identify with different parts of the political spectrum. For example, the Transition Movement's goal of fostering low-energy economic re-localization efforts can be viewed as radical because it promotes profound social innovation in the realms of environmental sustainability, social justice, and participatory democracy. It even seeks to foster workable community-based economic alternatives like producer and consumer cooperatives to supplant or even eliminate community dependence on giant global corporations. This is not a conventionally liberal outlook, and few career Democrats at the national level support such a program.

There is a principled conservative constituency for the Transition Movement's vision. Many Jeffersonians, a political movement associated with Thomas Jefferson but still in existence, support small farms and businesses, resource conservation, simple living, an ethos of community self-reliance, and local democracy. They often support a profound shift away from our current social values and away from rigid, top-down, mega-solutions that are not plausible solutions. As Transition fellow-traveler Pat Murphy notes, the dominant modernist "values of novelty, comfort, convenience, ease, fashion, indulgence, luxury and competition along with other indolent values associated with declining empires [that] must give way to different values such as cooperation, temperance, prudence, moderation, conviviality, and charity."[45] All of this runs counter to core elements of the globalized vision of neoliberal corporate capitalism.

According to Gorringe and Beckham: "Not aligned to any political party, Transition works to change the cultural story, to make unelectable policies electable, to lead by example and action rather than by hectoring.... it seeks practical, realizable steps here and now which ordinary people can take to make society more resilient."[46]

The Stages of Transition Organizing

How do local Transition Initiatives organize to reshape their communities? There are at least three interactive stages in process at the local level.

The first stage of Transition organizing usually involves a local initiating group forming and hosting a number of public awareness-raising and community-dialogue events about:

- the serious threats to our local communities due to the combination of climate change, resource limits, and economic dysfunction, and

- the positive potential of creating a revitalized local community that is energy-lean, but also time-rich, less stressful, healthier, and happier.

The second stage of Transition organizing usually involves Transition organizers supporting existing groups and encouraging the formation of new community groups and projects that focus on community-resilience efforts. These may include creating local currencies; organizing buy-local campaigns; expanding bike paths; and setting up farmers markets, food coops, and community gardens. Some local Transition Initiatives have started or promoted local credit unions as an alternative to for-profit banks owned by distant corporations. They have also supported or started other locally-owned, often cooperatively-run, businesses engaged in substituting locally produced goods and services for corporate imports.

The third stage of the organizing model encourages the increasingly inspired and well-organized community to begin working together to create a detailed and comprehensive "Resilience Action Plan." The main task here is to help the local community develop an inclusive process for creating a well-vetted 20- to 25-year plan for how all sectors of the community can further re-localize the economy, mitigate against the worst impacts of global climate disruption, lower their energy needs, and move completely away from fossil fuels, as well as dangerous alternatives like nuclear energy, while enhancing the quality of life for all its residents. The topics that are usually covered in these plans include: food and farming, medicine and health, education, local economic production and distribution, fair trade, transportation, energy, housing, and the heart and soul of community life.

These three stages of Transition organizing, which are already visible in many local communities, will likely lead to fourth and fifth stages that have not yet been fleshed out but may well be necessary for the movement to reach its long-range goals.

But each community is different. Transition Initiatives may not move along as quickly and smoothly as the examples described above, or follow the same trajectory.

For example, Charlotte, Vermont, is mostly a wealthy rural town of about 4,500 people that doesn't have much commercial enterprise. Many people there do not yet feel the need for a resilient local economy and community. There still has been a lot of activity — re-skilling workshops, a resource directory, vegetable gardens on public land, etc. There has been general interest in Transition, as evidenced by our growing e-mail list.

Other Transition organizers live and work in struggling urban neighborhoods where people are hard-pressed to rebuild a local economy that is sustainable, just, and resilient. Transition work is about building a foundation that will be in place whenever the need is widely felt. Social movements take time and commitment to grow. What is great about this movement is that we can have fun and get to know our neighbors better while we do the work, whatever the nature of our community.

The experience of finding a joyful community is replicated again and again when people are asked why they are drawn to the Transition Movement. What the Transition Movement has to offer the faith community is its belief that a diverse group of people can come together with a desire for a resilient community without letting their differences halt their progress.

There are resources available, including books, films, and websites. There are workshops that help people begin an Initiative, maintain an Initiative, or to learn to be a trainer. There's a clear plan of action, though there are many variations from community to community or culture to culture. There are Transition Towns, Transition Neighborhoods, and even Transition Streets. Transition Ibiza, Spain, is an island Transition Initiative in the Mediterranean Sea.

We can best learn about Transition from the stories of people who are involved in the Movement. They are people who are excited and motivated by the possibility that they can really make a difference in their communities. Next we hear from some of those people.

Dinner at the first All-France Transition Conference,
in June 201 at La Fete de la Transition Apres Petrole
(*photo by Ruah Swennerfelt*)

CHAPTER 4
STORIES FROM TRANSITION
EVOLVING VISION AND STRATEGY

Blessed art Thou, O Lord our God, King of the world who makes the fruit of the tree.

Blessed art Thou, O Lord our God, King of the world whose word makes all things on earth.

Blessed art Thou, O Lord our God, King of the world who brings food out of the earth.

Blessed art Thou, O Lord our God, King of the world who gives clothes to cover our bodies.

Blessed art Thou, O Lord our God, King of the world who makes sweet smelling wood and plants.

Blessed art Thou, O Lord our God, King of the world who has kept us alive until now so we may find joy in what has just come to us.

Blessed art Thou, O Lord our God, King of the world who has created the wonderful things of earth and heaven.

—Hebrew prayer[47]

Psychologist Mary Pipher says that "people avoid facing problems they have no idea how to solve."[48] We live in such a time of stress, uncertainty, and chaos that it's understandable that many people want nothing more than to hunker down in their homes, avoiding the truth of the state of the world.

We often hear people ask, "What can I, just one person, do?" Wen Stephenson says, "We face an unprecedented situation—a radical situation. It demands a radical response."[49] How do we find what that radical response is, except by relying on each other?

53

The Transition Town Movement touches the very pulse of our uncertainty by providing a lifeline. Its success lies in the very simple notion that by working together with neighbors, friends, and family we can find hope, love, and meaning.

Author Barbara Kingsolver so aptly says, "It's love for my homeland that obliges me to participate in the discussion of preserving its integrity, and to take any risk necessary on my country's behalf."[50]

When people involved in Transition Towns are asked what their primary motivation was to join or start a Transition Initiative, they say, because "it's fun" or "it's positive." It is no surprise that these ideas are emphasized during Transition training. Most people don't want to add yet another meeting to their busy schedules, but if they are drawn to a gathering where food and fun are part of their time together, they tend to come back. The truth of this has been witnessed again and again at the burgeoning Transition Initiatives around the world, which are demonstrated by the stories in this chapter.

Klaus Harvey, Hilda Ryan-Purcell, Jeannie Timony, and Liz Creed
(*photo by Ruan Swennefelt*)

Transition Town Kinsale, Ireland

Liz Creed, Klaus Harvey, Hilda Ryan-Purcell, and Jeannie Timony are proud that they were part of the beginnings of Transition during Rob Hopkins' time in Kinsale. In addition to being very kind to me, as I wrote in My Journey, they shared about Transition Town Kinsale. Here is some of what I learned from them.

Transition Town Kinsale's 12-member steering committee meets every three weeks. Their e-mail list has 250 names. There are 9 to 10 subcommittees, which were originally organized out of a 2009 open-space event. According to Rob, about 30 percent of the town population really know and understand about Transition, and 60 to 70 percent have at least heard about it.

In 2011, Transition Town Kinsale was awarded a €10,000 feasibility study grant to determine whether a community-run anaerobic digester was financially viable as a way to convert locally produced farm waste into locally used energy. And it concluded, "Yes, it is." Next, a much larger grant was awarded to help develop a complete business plan, including the identification of farm waste providers, fuel converters, digester technology providers, sources of finance, operating plan, etc.

In early 2012 the plan was completed. The project was shown again to be viable in financial, environmental, and energy production terms. Farmers, financial and legal experts, local business owners, technology providers, fuel converters, waste providers, fuel users, and local residents have become involved in the project.

When established, this will be the only community-run project of its kind in the country, saving farmers thousands of pounds per year on chemical fertilizer and reducing the miles that food waste needs to trucked to a landfill. It also improves soil and water quality. By providing local employment it retains up to €700,000 in the local economy that had been going elsewhere. In short it's fabulously sustainable!

Each autumn, Transition Town Kinsale throws a Food Fest & Harvest Celebration. This includes food concessions, a café, and a "5-mile competition" for locally grown food. At the end of the day they hold a concert. In the spring they sponsor a Spring Fair, which is a major fundraiser with workshops. Also, they hold annually a Sow & Grow seed swap with workshops. Two members set up a Community-supported Agriculture CSA), using the Transition network, and now it is operating independently. There's a second

CSA, supported by Transition Town Kinsale, for oats, quinoa, and potatoes, which provides "veg bags" for members (weekly bags of food). The grains are an experiment to help create a stronger local food supply.

Through such creative events and projects, Transition Town Kinsale has served as an exciting model of countless other Transition Initiatives that have sprung up across Europe and other parts of the world.

Transition Town Trieves, France

The first All-France Transition Conference, La Fete de la Transition Apres Petrole, was held in June 2011. Transition Town Totnes, in England, sent Naresh Giangrande to support the conference as well as the special celebration of Transition Trieves becoming an official Transition Initiative.

At the conference there was a large map of France, and people had put up stickers to show where they came from. Most of France was represented. Two of the initiators of Transition Trieves, Pierre Bertrand and Jeremy Light, were there. Jeremy, a biologist, had a revelation 50 years ago about the global environmental crisis while doing research in Antarctica, and he has worked on environmental issues ever since. He came to Trieves from England to work at an ecological center, Terre Vivante (Living Earth). Jeremy said he saw Transition as a logical movement to enhance the work he was already doing. He would like to see Trieves be much more locally reliant and believes that's the essence of being resilient. He avoided any prescription of what a Transition Initiative should be, instead encouraging many different initiatives. He too described the Transition Movement as spreading like a virus around the planet. It's very broad in scope and invites all to join in.

Pierre learned about the peak oil phenomenon about 2004 and realized it was a crucial problem for our society. He had been active with a number of environmental groups, and he was disappointed in their usual, activist approach. Then, when he read Rob Hopkins' book, *The Transition Handbook*, he said, "This is it. Because here there were many things that could help us transition rather quickly. And Jeremy and I decided to found it in Trieves." He said he believes their valley is ripe for Transition—that it can be an energy-producing place in addition to an agricultural place. There's a rich, cultural life in the villages, and people have strong relationships to one another. Instead of supermarkets, there are many small shops. The evidence of the success of their efforts is clear: In 2010 there were 12 to 15 initiating groups, and by 2011 there were more than 50 throughout France. Trieves is part of the global food market, and what is produced there is not consumed locally; Pierre wants to see that reversed. Now 40 percent of the population work outside of the region, and he'd like to see more people working locally. Pierre said he's impressed with how many people around the globe are working on solutions, but they are working within the dominant economic system, which is leading us to hard times. "The Transition Movement can bring people together before they start fighting one another."

Transition Monteveglio, Italy

Cristiano Bottone, Silvia Neri, and Massimo Giorgini are members of Transition Monteveglio, Italy. Although Monteveglio is a rural town of about 5,000 people on the outskirts of the metropolitan area of Bologna, much of their Transition thinking includes the greater Bologna area. Some successes for them have included entering into a strategic partnership with local politicians and helping a new school go solar. They are also developing geothermal energy, which will provide energy not only for the school but also for the town. In addition to the usual presentations of talks

(from left) Massimo Giorgini, Silvia Neri, and Cristiano Bottone
Transition Monteveglio, Italy
(*photo by Ruah Swennerfelt*)

and films and food, they are retrofitting old buildings to be more energy-efficient. In the fall of 2014 they were focused on "perma-transition," providing well-attended workshops on permaculture and how it applies to more than food.

Massimo has two reasons for working with Transition Monteveglio. First, he thinks that Earth needs our work and our creativity to solve the problems. Second, the Transition Movement is the first environmental movement he has encountered that is interested in Inner Transition and in the need for change of our consciousness. "We must first change ourselves to change the world." Also, he says, the Transition process helps people express themselves, empowers people to change the world, and gives people hope. Massimo's wife, Silvia Neri, says she is drawn to the Transition Movement because she appreciates its participatory style, where everyone can take part, where everyone can share their talents, and where everyone can find their way. She likes know-ing that she doesn't need to do everything—that people share in the work. She's excited about changing the current individualistic orientation of society to one more focused on community. Learning about permaculture touched something deep inside her, and so it was a natural for her to work in the Transition Movement.

Cristiano, a Transition trainer, works in advertising, and from that point of view he saw the truth of what is happening in the world, which advertising often serves to obscure. His life was changed by learning what Rob Hopkins was doing in England—how to be less controlling and how to allow people to bring their own energies and ideas into a collaborative process. He also saw how much fun people were having while doing this important, but often tiring, work. He found it was easy to encourage others to join. As he began to import the Transition process to Italy, one problem he faced was the fact that all the Transition books were in English. Once he and others of the core group started translating the materi-als into Italian, more people were becoming involved and feeling welcome.

Massimo's vision for greater Bologna includes another way to collaborate, to fully communicate, to go beyond the false separa-tions that language sometimes creates. He draws people's attention away from surface differences to their common goal of a beautiful and peaceful city with clean air, clean water, and clean streets. He emphasizes that they have a unique opportunity to be an example for the rest of Italy because they represent an important historic and geographic region.

Silvia's vision is all about communication. She wants to see many Transition groups in every part of the city and in every street. She wants a city where people naturally go into the streets to talk with one another. She wants to see more people walking and biking about, because when people are in cars, they don't communicate with each other. Massimo and Silvia bike to work, despite the risks of venturing out into a car-filled city without many bike lanes. She's tired of all the cement and envisions more green spaces.

Cristiano notes that Bologna is a town where many revolutions have been started, and so he believes it's ripe for a new type of revolution. Politicians and cooperatives in Monteveglio are very interested in what is happening. There are ten Transition Initiatives in Italy, and he believes this idea can be planted throughout the country.

Massimo believes that Italy, home of an earlier renaissance, can use that model for a new renaissance for a global vision. Silvia thinks it's important for everyone to work locally but always with a global vision in mind.

There's already a global vision for big change, according to Cristiano. People are trying to make changes but making little progress because they're using the old system, which is good at squelching new ideas. He believes that systemic change is necessary, as inspired by Donella Meadows' work on systems thinking. Cristiano believes that thinking "outside the box" creates new possibilities, because it connects with creative people just waiting for the opportunity to participate. He believes the global vision is already there, we just have to tap into it. Cristiano talked about the "people who are standing outside the open door" of the Transition Movement, not knowing whether to walk in. He talked about being patient, continuing to set the example, excite them, and show them how much fun it is to work with the group. Eventually some will cross the threshold. Cristiano said one woman took one and a half years, after standing at the sidelines, to walk in. As I listened to the stories, my spirit soared. My next meeting with a Transition organizer began in a forest.

Transition Tervuren, Belgium

Marc Van Hummelen is a forest ranger in Tervuren, Belgium, just outside of Brussels. Tervuren is a municipality in the province of Flemish Brabant, one of the three regions of Belgium. Marc works for Royal Donation, a government organization for natural areas that is required to provide its own financing, receiving revenues from logging and renting buildings among other things. Marc works at an arboretum and at an adjacent managed forest that covers about 400 hectares (about 1,000 acres). His job is part enforcement and part maintenance and upkeep of the forest. He is provided half of a very grand old house on the premises where he lives with his wife and three children. The other ranger lives in the other half. It's a glorious setting, and he very much appreciates the gift of place and work. Our walk through the forest was very grounding for me after so much time spent in cities and on trains and buses.

Marc Van Hummelen
(*photo by Ruah Swennerfelt*)

At a "Transition Café" held in Marc's home, people gathered to talk about Transition, sustainability, and personal choices. When he moved to the forest, feeling lucky to live there, Marc made a commitment to himself to try to make a difference for the environment. In 2008, he was already working with several environmental organizations, including a pre-order food cooperative, when he read *The Transition Handbook*. Marc took the lead and organized a first gathering, which was an informal discussion about peak oil and climate change. About 45 people attended. Others joined Marc, and they began showing documentaries. Five serve on the core team, and three of them have taken the Transition training. There are about 110 people on the e-mail list. They held several workshops, on candle making, preserving food, and alternative ways of eating. They also sponsored "24 hours without electricity."

Transition Café in Tervuren, Belgium
(*photo by Ruah Swennerfelt*)

For Marc, the Transition Movement is a synthesis of other activities that he was already part of. Those activities were all from the same perspective of creating a better environment, but the programs acted independently, without much communication. He had talked to people about creating an umbrella organization, but it didn't catch on. Then he found Transition. It was just what he was looking for. As an organizer of the movement, he feels he treads on tough ground. He wants to make sure that he doesn't dominate the discussion or direction of the group. He avoids sharing what is his own vision, opting for a more powerful vision emerging from the collective whole.

He is living his own vision in his backyard, using permaculture, living simply, using a simple composting toilet, etc. He wants to see a "heart and soul" group created, but it hadn't happened yet. He said that is where the visioning will happen. Marc is both optimistic and pessimistic about a world vision. He sees initiatives popping up all over the place, but he also sees a few billion people who are oblivious to the problems and the need for change. Overall he's pessimistic, but that is part of his drive to change things and to encourage more and more people to come to this Initiative. According to Marc, "If I was content with the world, maybe I wouldn't have helped start Transition Tervuren."

Isobel Vandermeulen
(*photo by Ruah Swennerfelt*)

Isobel Vandermeulen, present at Marc Van Hummelen's house, has had a long-standing concern for nature and animal rights, and upon finding Transition Tervuren she immediately wanted to join. She wanted to learn more about peak oil and climate change. But basically she joined because of her great concern for Earth and the raising of animals for food. So, vegetarianism and energy conservation are two of her main focuses. She'd like to learn how to live more in harmony with nature. She imagines a Tervuren where everything is local, "where we work locally, where we generate energy locally, where all shops are local, where we don't use cars to get around, where we create our food locally, where we learn together, and where we get to know each other again."

She would like to see the whole town as one vegetable garden. Although she hears that Belgium doesn't have enough land to feed its people, she doesn't believe it. She believes that if all the available land were used for food production, there would be enough. Isobel knows that the Transition idea is growing, and that other European countries are changing, but she feels that Belgium is not making the necessary changes and feels pessimistic about the future.

Olivier Bori, also at the Transition Café in Tervuren, is an Information Technologyspecialist and used to think that technology would solve the world's problems. But now he understands that there are better solutions, and he finds hope in the Transition Movement. He likes the focus on local and organic agriculture. Olivier said, "With the other people in the group you can work together, and with Transition you can change things." Before he came to Tervuren he was working with another environmental group, but it had no collective consciousness like that offered by Transition.

Olivier likes knowing that Transition is not political. Olivier's vision includes a citizenry with a changed understanding of what needs to be done to become resilient. It's a place where people ask each other for help to make the changes. He thinks people will change only if they are forced to, as when the people of Cuba had to change when oil supplies were no longer available because of the collapse of the Soviet Union. He hopes for a place where everyone enjoys their gardens and where true resili-

Olivier Bori
(*photo by Ruah Swennerfelt*)

ence is found. Olivier says that in his heart he has much hope for the future, but when he looks at what is going on he doesn't have that hope. "If you concentrate on negative things, you begin to be consumed by the negativity," he said. He would like things to change quickly, and looking back ten years, people didn't know about climate change, but in spite of the many lies from the government and others, people are learning the truth. Not long ago he was depressed about the fate of the world, but because of Transition and the people he is now working with, plus the fact that even some of his family members have made some changes, he has hope that the concepts will spread exponentially and that change is possible for the world.

Transition Tramore, Ireland

Paul Flynn's education is in environmental studies, and he was then a "Litter Warden," or environmental officer, for the Waterford City Council. He worked on issues of illegal dumping, etc., involving businesses and individuals. Transition Tramore began in 2008 and now has about 50 members. They held an energy show in 2009, which drew more than 4,000 people. They've had the traditional films and speaker events.

Paul was drawn to the Transition Movement because it is very inclusive. He also appreciated that *The Transition Handbook* was not a document "sealed in stone," but that you can take from it what you want, what makes sense for your town. He liked the localization approach, which is where we'll have to go to survive a post-fuel economy and climate change.

Paul's vision for Tramore includes energy independence and healthy employment. He'd like to see more tourists coming in and to be prepared for a future of more "stay-cations" — staying near to where you live for your vacations. "I want a strong, resilient community in Tramore where we can help each other, support each other, and have the tools to do that," said Paul. People are beginning to grow their own food, and many good things are already happening. Paul added, "I suppose if there's a few key words,

Paul Flynn
(photo by Ruah Swennerfelt)

say, they would be resilient, safe, and friendly."

His emphasis on community comes from his own experience when he was about eight years old, when his father was on strike for two years from the paper mill where he worked. They had no money. He remembers his mom cooking on the small wood-fired heater because their utilities were cut off. The support of their neighbors, a cup of sugar showing up, or some cooked food brought by, is an incredibly powerful memory for Paul. Although they were financially destitute, they didn't feel alone. He hopes that same level of neighborliness will grow out of the Transition Movement.

Paul thinks that people don't really feel how big the problem is. He says that definitely there is a global vision growing. Just the fact of how the Transition Movement has grown shows that there is change happening. He appreciated my work to help build the web, because it's so easy to feel separated from others in the movement. Transition Tramore promoted a 350.org event, planting ten trees, which brought in many new people. He thinks this proves that there are great movements happening and there are great opportunities to unite in the work. The future looks bright because more people in Tramore are getting out of their homes and engaging with others in the town—Paul's vision of a caring neighborhood.

Transition Alingsås, Sweden

Anton Adreasson, a member of Transition Alingsås, was born and grew up in Alingsås (about 45 kilometers, or 30 miles, from Göteborg/Gothenburg). After a ten-year period of living in Göteborg, he returned in 2010 with his wife and son. He and his wife do not own a car, but occasionally borrow his parents' car, which his wife drives because Anton has never had a driver's license. Upon returning to his hometown, he joined Transition Alingsås, which was started in 2009. There are five to ten people (depending on the day) on the core team. They host Transition Cafés every Monday evening, and about 10 to 15 people attend. Sometimes they host a speaker at the Café. They host a "Ning" site (a social network), which has 72 members, and have a website.

Anton Adreasson meeting with me in a café
(*photo by Louis Cox*)

In 2008 students from a university outside of Alingsås completed a research project about the city's potential sustainability. In 2011 Transition Alingsås, Passivhus Centrum, and a consortium of local NGOs invited local government council members and representatives of the various local political parties to review the students' research results and to discuss a sustainable Alingsås for the future. About 100 people attended the lively and informative session.

Transition Alingsås has hosted study circles on the topics of peak oil, growth, and small farms. They have also offered workshops on keeping bees, preserving food, and pickling. This year they were invited to be the local organization responsible for a small plot in a city park. They decided to showcase an edible garden. My cousin Eva, who lives in Alingsås, and I visited the garden, and we were very impressed with the bounty to be found in such a small area.

Anton's interests in nature began early in life, when he joined an organization dedicated to encouraging youth field biologists that was run only by youths. He participated in this organization from the age of 15 until he was 25. The main question about making real changes always ground to a halt because there never was enough money. He helped organize another environmental group in Göteborg and kept asking why they didn't have enough money to do what was important. He recognized that the international economic system, one focused mainly on profits, was the root cause of the problem. He also recognized that trying to change that system would be nearly impossible. He was attracted to the Transition Movement because it was doing something concrete, locally, and offered something that could create change. He also felt that being in a small city enhances the possibility of having an impact.

According to Anton, Sweden is dependent on oil imported from Denmark and Norway, two countries that soon will only have enough oil for themselves. The only other country that could supply oil is Russia, and they've just installed a pipeline to China; Anton is certain that China will outbid Sweden for that oil. In 2011 this crisis was not being talked about enough in public, but it was a huge issue for the energy future of Sweden. It would affect everything. Sweden is an importing country, importing a huge amount of products as imbedded energy. Now in 2016 Sweden is on a quest to be the first oil-free nation.

"Our dependency on oil should be broken by 2020," said Mona Sahlin, former minister of Sustainable Development for Sweden, in an interview with *The Guardian* newspaper. "There shall always be better alternatives to oil, which means no house should need oil for heating, and no driver should need to turn solely to gasoline."

Anton's vision is for a healthy post-petroleum economy and community. The main issue for Anton is to offer a common awareness of the issue. He doesn't have the solution, but he feels that each group will find its own solutions. Anton believes a local focus rather than a national focus will be the key to a successful transition.

Anton said that in Sweden they have a good history of well-educated people being drawn to environmental organizations and work, but it's hard to bring the masses to the understanding of what is needed. It's always the same people. The Transition idea holds out hope for a global movement. He added that focusing on Transition is better than focusing on a movement. "Stay focused locally, keep it leaderless, allow the ideas for change to emerge from the people, all of them."

Transition Heathrow, England

Not all Transition Initiatives are in cities or towns. One of the more unusual sites for a Transition Initiative is at Heathrow Airport outside of London, England, where people are squatting on the site of a proposed new runway. Transition Heathrow was established because local folk were outraged that Heathrow was proposing to create yet another runway, which would increase air and noise pollution and grab land being used for agriculture. From the Transition Heathrow website:

> "We hope to bring to light the environmental damage and misery future airport expansion at Heathrow will bring to local residents and businesses. Our objective is to build permanent and sustainable communities within threatened areas to offer and show a viable alternative to the bulldozing of green spaces, houses, lives and history."[51]

Some of the actions of Transition Heathrow include community gardens, re-skilling workshops, regular gatherings, films, and health classes. Transition Heathrow is still under threat of eviction. But as this book goes to press in March 2016, they have been given a stay of execution as the court was adjourned until summer, 2016. Still the bailiffs could arrive unannounced at any time. This threat will continue, unless the landowner lets them buy the land.

Transition Brasilandia, Brazil

A question often asked is whether a Transition Initiative can exist in an economically challenged community, where the struggle for daily survival often overrides having energy for building community. In fact, one of the Initiatives in Brazil is located in Brasilandia, a low-income district of São Paulo. In August of 2009 an international Transition Training in São Paulo generated three Transition Initiatives. There were challenges to the idea that the global North would have something to offer when so many sustainable projects were already underway. But they soon came to realize that the structure of Transition did have a lot they could build on. Then there was a Transition training in Rio de Janeiro, where several more initiatives were founded, including Brasilandia.

Isabela de Menezes is a member of Transition Granja Viana, near São Paolo, and has many contacts with Transition Brasilandia. She explained that in Brasilandia there are many subsections of the slum, each with a name and a sense of pride of place by its inhabitants. At the edge of Brasilandia is the biggest urban forest in the world, which supplies 80 percent of the water for São Paulo.

Isabela de Menezes, Transition Granja Viana, Brazil
(*photo by Ruah Swennerfelt*)

A huge part of the Transition education is about the value of the forest, and they are "moving the forest into the city," transplanting trees into yards and trying to stop development encroaching on the forest. In addition they are reviving stories of the history of Brasilandia to share in the schools and growing edible gardens on school property. Other projects include zero-waste efforts. They've mapped where waste lies in large heaps around the area, removed it very publicly, and encouraged people not to continue to throw waste in these areas but only at designated places.

Transition Paris, France

Since Transition is all about connection, resilience, and community, how is it possible to have a Transition Paris, or Barcelona? It is daunting to think of trying to support a Transition Initiative in a city of 10.5 million people living in the greater Paris area, with 2.3 million living in the city. People involved with Transition Paris see the possibilities.

Ralph Boehlke, Transition Paris
(*photo by Ruah swennerfelt*)

Ralph Boehlke, a member of Transition Paris, says that although there are several Transition Initiatives in various districts, people in Paris often associate across district lines, which makes it more challenging. Ralph has been a part of an anti-globalization movement that has a reputation for being aggressive and only mentioning what was wrong. When Ralph came across the Transition Movement, he was thrilled that it took all the wrong into account, but was proposing an alternative. Paris is reported to be the most densely populated city in the world. Paris is not resilient and doesn't have the capability to be a buffer for anything. Paris has to create more spaces, more green spaces for growing things and for breathing space. He would also like to see streets with fewer cars. Relationships among neighbors are almost non-existent. Rooftop gardens are impossible because most of the roofs are slanted. Also lacking are places for people to gather. This could be achieved by making some streets only for pedestrians. Ralph sensed a general unhappiness, but the people don't know how to put a name on it. He wants to put words to it, so the unhappiness can be defined as a first step, including imagining the Transition for Paris.

In 2014, there were six Transition Initiatives in and close to Paris. Since there is a focus on "Transition Streets" and "Transition Neighborhoods," it expands the networks of the rural areas and small towns into the cities.

Transition Los Angeles, USA

According to their brochure, Transition Los Angeles, in another dauntingly huge city, was established in late 2008 as a city hub to support the blossoming of Transition ideas among the residents of Los Angeles. Local initiatives have sprouted up across the greater Los Angeles basin, with more forming.

Joanne Poyourow has been a part of Transition Los Angeles since its beginning. She was also a blogger on the Transition US website when I met her. She was involved in starting a small community garden with flowers and vegetables that was created on the lawn of a church. The church wanted to make the change from lawns to food, and there was a ready set of hands in the neighborhood to do the work.

Joanne said many people ask her, "Which comes first, the local group or the hub?" For Los Angeles the hub came first, because at the first Transition training the 19 participants came from all over the area, and they felt they needed a support system to keep the momentum going.

Joanne Poyourow, Transition Los Angeles
(*photo by Ruah Swennerfelt*)

At the very beginning, in late 2008, Mar Vista/Venice, Westchester, and Culver City neighborhoods were groups in formation. As of 2014 they had 12 active pods. Early on, they made a decision not to localize by geographic area, but instead by where people felt a sense of belonging. On their website there are individuals identified in certain areas who are looking for others to work with. What a great networking tool that is!

Transition Los Angeles has a leadership team of 28 people, holds monthly meetings, and is connected electronically. They have at least one representative from each pod (an earthy, permaculture approach to naming the Initiatives), although not everyone can come to every meeting. The work of the individual Los Angeles Transition Initiatives is very localized. The hub acts as a facilitating device and uses its ability to bring in important speakers and host larger events. The hub helps when local groups encounter leadership issues, or need some guidance.

Joanne is excited by how fast it's growing and how individualized each pod is. The challenge is the size of the area. The leadership team doesn't look at the big picture very often. They don't think about the fact that there are 11 million people out there and worry that most of them don't know about Transition. Instead they "put one foot in front of the other" and stay focused on what they can do. Joanne said this is better than doing nothing, and it's also moving them in the right direction.

Joanne was attracted to the Transition model because she feels it's about the only model that can address the combined issues of peak oil, climate change, economic contraction, and social injustice. It involves all the petals of the permaculture flower. In fact, Joanne published a novel, *Legacy*, about using permaculture as an inspiration for humans to transition from an oil-based culture to one without cheap oil. Just before publication she found Rob Hopkins's work and realized that all the way across the planet someone else came to the very same conclusions! She also said that she couldn't imagine doing anything else with her life.

Her vision for Los Angeles is what her book covers. For the book she had created a time-line for success. Now that the Transition Movement is active, she has seen that constructed time-line shorten for the positive changes of Transition, and that excites her. One vision includes food gardens permeating the whole area. She now sees that the food base is happening so much faster than she ever imagined.

She believes that the world vision is what is coming out of Rob Hopkins's work—that he is the "visioner." She also said that we are in a grieving phase and that the vision will only come after that phase. She also said that since being globalized is a contradiction to Transition, there really couldn't be a "world" vision. It must be made up of local visions that are human scale. Transition is one very meaningful path to a resilient future.

But why would specifically a person of faith search out the nearest Transition Initiative or encourage neighbors and friends to start one? What does that person have to offer a grassroots, local group? How does the Movement enrich one's faith journey? Stories from those people help us understand these questions. That is the subject of the next chapter.

CHAPTER 5
PEOPLE OF FAITH AND TRANSITION

Today we know that the relationship between the human species and the Earth is ill described by... metaphors of hierarchy. Not only do we know that what we breathe in depends upon what the trees and grasses breathe out; now we know that within our own guts are myriads of microscopic creatures that occasionally make us sick but far more often keep us alive and healthy.

There is no 'environment' in the sense of an "environs" that is "out there," not us. There are fringes, not fences, between us and other life, and some-times not even fringes at our edges but in our very innards.

Though now we know the Human species has indeed great power to shape and damage the web of life on earth, we also know today that we are part of that web – a strand within it – not simply above and beyond it. What we may do to the web out of our unusual power also has an impact upon us. The more we act as if we are in total control, the closer we come to "totaling" the whole intricate process (to use a phrase that – perhaps not accidentally – comes from the world of automobiles.)

So those metaphors of ordered hierarchy are no longer truthful, viable, or useful to us as tools of spiritual enlightenment. If we are to seek spiritual depth and height, the whole framework of prayer must be transformed.
—Rabbi Arthur Waskow, "Prayer as if Earth Really Matters"[52]

Today, people of many faiths feel called to work creatively with their neighbors to foster a more spiritually fulfilling, socially just, and ecologically sustainable human presence on our planet. They see the global challenges we face—climate disruptions, mas-sive species extinctions, resource depletions, and an increasingly unsustainable and unjust global economy—and they want to do something meaningful in terms of the living principles of their faith traditions. This promising trend among religious congregations, often called the "greening of faith," has been well documented in a number of recent books, articles, and documentaries.[53]

The principles underlying the Transition Movement have a natural connection to spiritual understandings of caring for all of life on the planet. Transition communities begin and grow by getting people of all viewpoints and backgrounds together regularly for local-food potlucks, discussions about sharing resources and building resilience, listening to speakers and watching films, making music, and having fun as they explore how to really prepare for climate chaos and for the end of cheap, abundant fossil fuel.

What might that look like if those events were clearly welcoming to people from all faith traditions and interested in learning how they too can guide us in Transition work? Have people have been particularly inspired by their faiths to be part of Transition? Has their participation in Transition enhanced their experience with their faith communities? What have they brought back to their faith communities from their experiences in Transition?

There is great power when people of faith come together to fight for a cause, as we saw during the civil rights struggles in the United States. The photo below of Martin Luther King Jr. and Rabbi

Rabbi Abraham Heschel marching together with Martin Luther King, Jr.
(photo by John C. Goodwin, used with permission)

Abraham Heschel marching together inspires us all to reach out, not only to people of varying faiths, but across all the perceived divides, because we are all in this together. And together we will prevail. Today we see the same power in Hoda Baraka's photo on the front cover where people of many faiths came together in Rome to declare their care for Earth. The Transition Movement holds out this possibility, but it's up to us to make the dream come true.

Worldview and Faith Traditions

Some respondents expressed the sense that their faith-based worldviews diverge sharply from those that undergird much of Western civilization and are threatening the long-term health of the community of life. Being part of a sacred covenant with Creation stands in sharp contrast to the widely held assumption that Earth is essentially a collection of passive materials that were created to aid humans in their drive for material wealth and short-term profits.

What is meant by "worldview"? One's worldview may be thought of as a culturally acquired lens that helps us place our experiences in a larger context of time and place. Worldviews may be transmitted through social conditioning or as stories or scripts that frame our responses and decisions to life situations.

Our worldview is the story of our origins that we grew up with or adopted as adults. It informs the way we relate to Earth. Are we believers of having mastery over all that lives? Or are we believers in an evolving co-creation that we are part of? Has the dominant worldview of the Western world and its consumer culture completely taken over our thoughts and actions?

How could we change that worldview? When we understand how deep-seated and formative our worldviews are, it becomes clear that merely "reforming" lifestyles and institutions with the help of Earth-friendly laws and technologies will not make the way humans currently are using our Earth Mother sustainable. The "religion" of material progress will have to change radically. The impetus for such a change comes from the cascading crises that are steadily undermining the legitimacy of that prevailing worldview. But even in the throes of major social, economic, and ecological turmoil, most people aren't likely to let go of their current worldview until they are aware of an alternative worldview that makes more sense.

We can begin to imagine such a change at the planetary level only because of the transformation in worldview that many individuals have experienced. In his seminal essay "Thinking Like a Mountain," Aldo Leopold told of facing a crisis in his forestry career. He had become increasingly aware that the human-centered perspective underlying the contemporary conservation movement was too narrow, shortsighted, and ultimately destructive to the health and wholeness of the biotic community. He finally realized the way forward depended more on the development of a "bio-centric land ethic" than prohibitions against specific actions. He was calling for an awakening to an ecological consciousness that goes beyond intellectual understanding.[54]

Leopold's personal transformation has a lot in common with conversion experiences that many other people throughout history have reported in the context of organized religion. We can think of the radical reorientation the apostle Paul after his spiritual epiphany on the road to Damascus. Paul's experience did not involve abandonment of his religious tradition as much as it led to discovery of larger, underlying truths that needed new concepts and structures to given them expression.[55]

Similarly, when people today advocate for the "greening" of their respective faith traditions they are also challenging and reframing secular worldviews that have frequently accompanied those traditions. "Re-greening" might be a better term, since many of the great faith traditions were based on experiences in nature. But gradually as they became institutionalized and urbanized, they became disconnected from the natural world. "Sky gods" replaced the traditional sense of the immanence of Spirit in nature and introduced a profoundly dualistic worldview.

Many people of faith are recognizing that the dualistic thinking of "I am here and nature is out there" has led us down a path that is destroying so much of what is "out there" and harming ourselves as well. They believe that the Transition Movement, focused on the wholeness of resilient communities, will help change this worldview. Resilient communities are dependent on a strong natural environment, healthy ecosystems, and biodiversity. We need this resilience not just for humans' sake, but also because we recognize and respect the intrinsic value of all of life on the planet.

Today there are new prophets promoting ecological consciousness as a pathway to a sustainable future. The late Father Thomas Berry, a self-described "geologian," articulated a new worldview that integrates ancient spiritual wisdom with the evolutionary insights of leading-edge scientific thinking.[56] Transition Movement founder Rob Hopkins offers a model for living sustainably and joyously on Earth through the integration of permaculture principles, new-wave economics, and egalitarian communities. Thomas Berry and Rob Hopkins are not offering final answers but are inviting both secular reformers and people of faith to explore the blessed awareness of moving with the rhythms of nature instead of fighting against them.

Faith-Based Groups and Transition

In 2013, Timothy Gorringe, a British theology professor, and Rosie Beckham, a student from the University of Exeter, wrote a groundbreaking pamphlet called *The Transition Movement for Churches: A Prophetic Imperative for Today*. The authors' main goal was to encourage more British Christians to get involved in the Transition Movement, the visionary community-organizing effort that had spread rapidly around the United Kingdom and the world since it first took root in Totnes, England.[57]

While the Transition Movement appeals to many different people, not just Christians or other people of faith, Gorringe and Beckham argued that Transition organizing is a great way for Christians to put their faith into action. They saw Transition organizing as a powerful way to love our neighbors and God's good Earth in a world-changing way—several local communities at a time.

> "The attraction of the Transition Movement is that it rests on practical and local initiatives to meet the challenges, not only of peak oil, but also of climate change and the ongoing financial and economic crisis. More importantly, both active Christian citizens and Transition organizers believe 'that a more satisfying, creative and community-oriented way of life can be found than we currently experience.' Christians have much to offer such a movement and have much to learn and gain as well."[57]

The Rev. Peter Sawtell of Eco-Justice Ministries

The Rev. Peter Sawtell wrote, "Facing up to the global eco-justice crisis is good for the church." He then listed three ways that it was good:

1) It is an occasion to revisit scripture and theology.

2) It affirms to the world that we have an important moral witness.

3) It is an opportunity for us to announce good news.

"When so many voices around us are saying that our culture can't change, or that change requires suffering and deprivation, we can lift up an invitation to a different and richly satisfying life of abundance, community and responsibility. That's a good message for the world, and it is good for the church when we can provide real good news. If we can lift up that message, it might even entice new people to come to church!"[58]

Rabbi Arthur Waskow of the Shalom Center in Philadelphia, Pennsylvania

Rabbi Arthur Waskow, in a blog published in December 2014, went a step further than most climate activists in describing the work ahead of us. This was written after a young African-American man was held in a chokehold by the police, all the while calling out, "I can't breathe." He died on the street while the police looked on. After that horrible act of violence, a rallying call went out using "I can't breathe" as the mantra. Rabbi Waskow went a step further than the issue of one man.

"[The cure] will come when we turn away from domination and toward community; when white, black, and brown citizens join in haunting police departments until every police officer who kills an unarmed civilian is fired; when neighbors gather at local coal-burning plants wearing gas masks and sit in the gateways to force an end to the epidemic of asthma that afflicts our poorer, blacker, disempowered neighborhoods; when all across our country, neighborhood co-ops are producing solar energy; when churches, synagogues, mosques, and their congregants are choosing to 'move our money,' placing our savings and checking accounts with credit unions and neighborhood banks, not megabanks that invest in destroying mountains to burn coal, killing the oceans to drill for oil, poisoning our ground water to profit from unnatural gas. When these kinds of communities start growing and sprouting at the grassroots and pavement tops of our country, we will see new laws sprouting through new cracks in the rigid concrete of our top-down governments."[59]

Ibrahim Abdul-Matin

Ibrahim Abdul-Matin, a Brooklyn-based Muslim, argues that it is not wise for any modern movement, including the environmental movement, to become "oversecularized" and discourage thousands and potentially millions of people from becoming active participants.[60] Abdul-Matin also quotes Muslim environmental author Seyyed Hussein Nasr, saying that too many promising movements have had a secular leftist "tendency with a tone decisively opposed to established religions." He gives the following text from the Quran as an inspiration to not harm what God has created:

> "So Set your face steadily and truly to the Faith: (establish) Allah's handiwork according to the pattern on which he has made mankind: No change (let there be) in the work (wrought by Allah: that is the true Religion: But most among mankind understand not."[61]

George Owen: Transition Greater Media

A "Great Unleashing" of a Transition Initiative occurs after the Initiative has been working for a period of time, sometimes several years, and its members feel that the wider community needs to be invited to learn and participate in the exciting process of becoming resilient. Media, Pennsylvania has a population of 6,000, but Transition Greater Media serves a population of 30,000. One part of Transition Greater Media is Transition Cheltenham. I attended their Great Unleashing in April 2011.

George Owen of Transition Greater Media recognizes the challenge of nurturing community where all are encouraged to engage with others in their community, doing the things that they do. Some may not be interested, or may be suspicious of the Transition Movement. But, he says, meet them and get to know them where they are.

> "I believe that it is dealing with people who don't share the same interests with you that is the most productive for change. If you always have people who are like-minded, or like-interested, you aren't creating community yet. Parker Palmer says, 'Community is the one place where the one person you don't want to live with, lives.'

> "I was attracted to the Transition Movement because of its emphasis on positive vision and its community focus. I did not see hope in working to change big government because it is so corporately controlled. Transition Towns offered a positive alternative and it encourages our doing the work joyfully. Bringing joy to what we do is a central piece of what we do on earth. I believe that this movement could work.

> "My global vision is one of increasingly larger circles of connection, from the individual community to the region, to a larger area, etc. To this end we are involved with all eastern Pennsylvania Transition work and promote Transition Towns among Quakers.

> "All of this is about learning to live with conflict. The core vision is radical acceptance and compassion, and the 'economics of happiness.'"

> "Compassion seems to be the foundation of working with people who think differently, are of different cultures, or are of different faiths, or no faith."

Maggie Flemming, Transition Sebastopol, California

Maggie Flemming of Transition Sebastopol, California, is a Buddhist and Earth-based ritual practitioner, and recently stepped down as co-director of Transition US.

Maggie Flemming
(*photo by Beverly Markiewicz*)

"I was drawn to Transition because of the movement's recognition of the need for an inner Transition in addition to an outer Transition. This inner Transition requires a change in worldview from being separate to being interconnected, a worldview that aligns with my orientation toward non-dualistic thinking." My Earth-based ritual work is a way to help people recognize and transcend dualistic thinking.

"I am a nonprofit leader working to build more resilient, equitable, and creative communities. The natural world has been one of my spiritual homes since I was a teenager. The feeling of stillness that I discovered in the wilderness was my first introduction to the stillness that I now also experience through meditation. Through my Buddhist practice, I have come to see the environment from a non-dualistic perspective. Rather than thinking about myself and the environment as separate, I hold the view that people and the environment are one.

"I had the opportunity to host two nature-based mindfulness events for my community this past year. My work with Transition has provided ideas for sharing with participants how these events fit into the broader context of building resilient communities. In many social-justice movements throughout history, faith communities have offered their expertise in good listening, in mediating issues, and in their belief in the goodness that exists in the world. They can offer their ability to maintain hope in the face of overwhelming obstacles. People of faith have a long history of facing and overcoming adversity.

"My faith has provided me a refuge from burnout. Working in the environmental movement, with the urgency to address climate change and economic instability, can be overwhelming. My meditation practice has been one way to practice self-care so that I have more energy to bring to my work with Transition US and Transition Sebastopol.

"Other elements of Buddhism that have informed my work include a beginner's mind and compassion. The Transition Movement is in itself a large-scale social experiment, which makes space for innovation and emergence. By cultivating a beginner's mind, an attitude of openness with a lack of preconceptions, I find that there's more opportunity to discover creative solutions for increasing resilience in our communities. The Buddhist emphasis on developing compassion ties in with my desire to support Transition groups to develop more sharing economies within their communities, such as, time banks, neighborhood exchanges, tool lending libraries, etc. It also informs my commitment to social justice work as part of the Transition movement."

How will the human race live as we enter the post-carbon world? Will Maggie's hope for non-dualistic thinking help make the necessary changes needed to avoid catastrophe? The interwoven planetary crises of our time are manifestations of a profound spiritual alienation from the source of life and health. While we must understand the spiritual basis of these crises and act from the heart, we must also learn practical ways to lessen the great suffering and disorientation that will result when cheap fossil fuels are no longer available for agriculture, transportation, and manufacturing, and when these activities are further hindered by climate chaos.

Thich Tri Quang, Buddhist Monk

The Venerable Thich Tri Quang, a Buddhist monk, is chief editor of *Gia'c Ngô*, a Buddhist magazine in Vietnam.

"Living in contentment does not mean the elimination of desire of knowledge and truth, but to live in harmony with all beings and with nature. On that basis, those who understand the Buddha's teaching will limit their selfishness, to live in harmony with nature without harming the environment. They will see what should be explored and to what level, what should be protected for future use by the next generations and other beings. Excessive greed to possess everything for themselves, or for their own group, has made men become blind. They are prepared to fight, make war, causing deaths, disease, starvation, destruction of life of all species, gradually worsening the living environment. By all means, they try to maximize their profits, without being concerned of the negative impact of unplanned exploitation leading to depletion of natural resources, discharge toxics into the air, water, earth, leading to environmental pollution, destroying the ecological balance."

Coalition on the Environment and Jewish Life

For Jews, the environmental crisis is a religious challenge. As heirs to a tradition of stewardship that goes back to Genesis and that teaches us to be partners in the ongoing work of Creation, we cannot accept the escalating destruction of our environment and its effect on human health and livelihood. Where we are despoiling our air, land, and water, it is our sacred duty as Jews to acknowledge our God-given responsibility and take action to alleviate environmental degradation and the pain and suffering that it causes. We must reaffirm and bequeath the tradition we have inherited which calls upon us to safeguard humanity's home.

Rabbi Katy Allen: Transition Wayland, Massachusetts

Rabbi Katy Allen, a co-founder of Transition Wayland, Massachusetts, shared that she was drawn to the Transition Movement because of its emphasis on gathering together neighbors to work on the issues of climate change and the other pressing concerns of the day. She saw it as a bridge between her work in her own faith community and the multi-faith community, as well as support for her work in her local community. Her evolving sense of having a deep connection to the larger Creation eventually led her to found a Jewish congregation, "Ma'yan Tikvah—A Wellspring of Hope," where the members celebrate Shabbat outdoors year around.

Wayland Walk focused on mushrooms, Transition Wayland, Massachusetts.
Rabbi Katy Allen is second from the right.
(*photo by Kaat Vander Straeten*)

"As a child I always had an important relationship with the outdoors. Those early outdoor experiences led me to become a high school science teacher. Over the years I have come to see myself less as a student of nature and more as a partner with nature, which I see in spiritual terms. My continuing love of the natural world is the foundation for my current faith-based work on environmental issues.

"My journey to Transition began when I had read an article in *Orion* magazine. A year or two after that, I saw that somebody was going to try to start a Transition group in Wayland where I live. I saw Transition as a way of bringing together my faith journey and my care about the environment. I didn't become a rabbi until about 11 years ago. So Transition has been part of my evolution, bringing all these pieces together. The whole issue of climate change had been on my mind for a long time. I have been on a journey to find out where my role is in the whole thing.

"All my work stems from my sense of spiritual connection to the universe. Judaism began as an indigenous religion, based on a sense of place and the agricultural cycles of the year. It is a rich resource that supports our inherent spiritual connection to the Universe. In Transition there is a place for this, the heart place. I lead Inner Transition workshops, as well as workshops dealing with the emotional and spiritual response to climate change in multi-faith contexts that have been supported by Transition Wayland."

I'm so inspired by the creativity found in each Transition Initiative. What people experiment with makes each place quite unique while still working for the same goals. This creativity is evidenced in what Katy brings to Transition Wayland as evidenced here.

"I have been offering 'Wayland Walks' at Transition Wayland. At a recent a full-moon walk I invited people to bring a poem or something else to share. I led a solstice gathering and people brought a fabulous combination of readings, which helped to raise the spiritual voice. It has been a mixture of my bringing things and inviting other people to bring things to these outings. Sometimes I have guided people in a meditation during these events. It depends on what it is. I'll tend to raise the spiritual voice if there's a place for it in the things we're doing.

"I wanted to have a place, where I could express my Jewish voice. That led me to found the Jewish Climate Action Network in the Boston area. There I found other people who were excited to find a Jewish organization dealing with climate change. During this period I moved from being a hospital chaplain to eco-chaplaincy. I also established a new project at Open Spirit in Framingham, a healing center. The One-Earth Collaborative focuses on our spiritual connection to

Earth and has programs around gardening, composting, and getting outdoors for walks and foraging, all with a spiritual twist.

"I like Transition because it's local. It's easier for me to be involved in issues with my community or the local clergy than on the national scale. I often bring news of what Transition is doing to the clergy association. At one point, Transition Wayland folks spoke at a clergy association gathering.

"Transition provides a place to be with everybody. We all share this Earth, whatever our belief. There are several ways that I engage with people about climate change: Jewish contexts, multi-faith or general spiritual contexts, and contexts with no definition of faith or spirituality as their core. The latter two apply to Transition and have given me opportunities to grow as a spiritual leader for all people in the context of climate change. Spirituality is always inherent in what I'm doing."

Ron Berezan Transition Powell River, British Columbia, Canada

Ron Berezan is an Anglican and a member of Transition Powell River in British Columbia, Canada. The connection to Transition Town work was a very natural step for Ron.

"I see Transition and permaculture as branches on the same tree. Transition excels in its offering of a methodology and strategy for bringing many of the core permaculture concepts and values into a community context. Permaculture brings with it many very specific technical approaches to achieving the goals of Transition. Together they can inspire communities to create a sustainable world.

"Growing up in the shadows of Vatican II in the late 60s and early 70s, I was blessed to have many visionary teachers, nuns, and priests in my life who passionately integrated deep concern for social justice and planetary well-being into their religious vision. One of my earliest catechismal memories is of a teacher saying to our class, 'God is everywhere, in all things, at all times.' Such reverence for the Divine immanence in all of life was a natural fit for a young child who spent countless hours climbing trees, exploring the forests, and peering into the ponds just beyond the last gravel road of my Edmonton, Alberta, middle-class neighborhood. Our place is within the natural world, not outside it.

"As an adult, I worked for many years for a variety of NGOs dedicated to social change and sustainable community development. I have always felt the desire to re-connect with a nurturing faith community but felt an equal amount of anxiety and trepidation about doing so, since I had become disillusioned with the emphasis on otherworldly salvation and redemption. I undertook a Master of Theology degree at a progressive United Church college in Edmonton,

(*above*) Transition Powell River members during the making of a garden.
Ron Berazan has his hand up.

(*below*) Ron Berazan is speaking at a dedication ceremony of an indigenous carving in the Transition Powell River permaculture garden.
(*both photos by Randy Murray*)

Alberta. While I had entered this program hoping to focus on the idea of 'compassion,' I soon abandoned that for a newfound fascination with the emerging 'eco-theology' movement and became deeply inspired by such writers as Thomas Berry (*The Universe Story*), Sally McFague (*The Body of God*), Rosemary Radford Reuther (*Gaia and God*) and a host of others. For my program practicum, I spent a month at Genesis Farm in New Jersey, working in their organic CSA (Community Supported Agriculture) program and participating in Creation-Centered Spirituality programs inspired by Thomas Berry and facilitated by Miriam McGillis.

"It was at Genesis Farm that I first encountered permaculture. Over the past 18 years, permaculture has become the most effective, natural, and inclusive way for me to bring together faith and practice, to unite these two worlds in a way that leaves me whole. Ten years ago, I left my NGO work to become a self-employed permacultural-ist — teaching, designing, and consulting on a myriad of interesting, transformative, and personally very meaningful projects throughout western Canada and in Cuba.

"Throughout my life, I believe my religious involvement and spiritual path have helped to ground me in some key existential questions: What is our deepest identity as humans? What is the nature of this Earth in which we live and the cosmos by which we are surrounded? How do we respond to the tremendous creative and destructive powers that are manifest all around us? How can we achieve right relationship with other beings, human and non-human alike? What should we consider sacred? It is not that my faith has provided answers to these questions, though it may attempt to; it is rather that it opens the door to their exploration.

"I believe that the nature of the cultural impasse we are facing today requires our willingness to ask some of these deeper questions. I don't believe we will find our way to a sustainable future by technical solutions alone, though they may have their place, but rather by a more fundamental reorienting of our institutions, our cultural patterns and our way of life.

"My faith journey has provided me with some of the tools to be able to engage folks at this core level of exploring our world views and some of our key assumptions about what it means to live a happy, fulfilling, and meaningful life. What kind of world do we want to live in? What are the cultural patterns and worldviews that have brought us collectively to where we are today and how can we envision a truly alternative future for all of life? I do believe that, as Joanna Macy describes, this is the 'Great Work' of our time and that, from a religious perspective, it is holy work, a sacred path, a vocation."

Ron's faith has helped him to understand that these changes cannot be undertaken alone—that it must be a community enterprise. He believes that his faith is a terrific fit with the Transition vision, which also aims to reconnect people to each other in very meaningful ways in the process of co-creating our future.

"We go forward together, or not at all. And rather than a descent into a somber and joyless future of deprivation, we are really talking about rediscovering how to fully embrace life, to awake from the slumber of individualistic consumerism and the isolation it has tainted us with, to become active and engaged members of vibrant communities. Even though Transition aims to awaken people to the folly of the path we are on, I like to frame it more as a seduction towards something better than a loss we have to endure.

"There have been many surprises as the permaculture work we are undertaking begins to slowly permeate the life of our congregation. There is a renewed sense of empowerment that we can have relevance to the community around us and that we can make some real concrete changes happen. An 'ecological consciousness' has begun to manifest itself more frequently into the prayers and ritual life of the community. There is a growing willingness of some of the elder members of our community to bring forth many of the manual skills they have practiced all their lives and they are valued by others for sharing those skills (gardening, food preserving, living simply, cooking, building things, etc.). I believe that, for at least some members of the congregation, there is an understanding that caring for Earth is a key component of our faith tradition and one that needs to be prioritized today.

"I have come to the understanding that churches represent a tremendously untapped opportunity for permaculture and Transition work. There is, in my opinion, a natural fit between the ethics of these movements and those of the mainline Christian Churches (i.e., peace, justice, and the integrity of Creation). Churches are generally underutilized physical spaces that can become lively community hubs. Indeed, they are among the very few remaining 'public' spaces within many of our communities. They can become sites for food gardens, for canning bees, for energy retrofits, for potlucks and picnics, for workshops and sharing circles, and for centers for organizing ourselves to deal with the emergencies or calamities that will undoubtedly continue to increase in the coming decades.

"My faith community, like most I suppose, is populated by folks with a whole range of opinions, politics, personalities, theologies, and priorities—a microcosm of society at large. Transition and permaculture have helped me to see the value in this diversity and the importance of finding ways for all to participate, for all to have their voices heard and to be invited to share the gifts that they bring to the table. This is by no means easy, but is a critical part of the journey in transitioning forward. Transition also teaches us that, although the way ahead is anything but certain, we need to make time for celebration and affirmation of all that we are creating together and of all the great blessings that the earth continues to offer us."

Many people of faith do have clear faith-based reasons for caring about the fate of the planet. This was evident by the thousands who gathered for the People's Climate March in New York City in September 2014. Packed together on 58th Street, waiting for hours before being able to join the march, were Buddhists, Ba'hai's, Unitarian Universalists, Jews, Pagans, Christians, Muslims, Hindus, and many others. All were united in their care for Creation and their concern for the human impact on the planet and all who dwell there. All were calling us to awaken to our complicity in this crisis and to undertake the necessary radical changes to leave a healthy, peaceful, and just planet for future generations. It was a moment of unity to be cherished and remembered.

Quaker Earthcare Witness

But what happens when those people of faith all return to their homes from such an exhilarating experience? How do they continue the momentum to work together? Quaker Earthcare Witness, an international NGO, emphasizes that real change will not occur unless we understand and know our deep psychic/spiritual connection to Earth, or as they say, to be in "unity with nature." So they see the important task is to help people recover that sense of belonging to the land not just living on it. The Transition Movement places great importance on the "heart and soul" of our relationship to the planet. Without it we'd lose the joy that is so apparent in all those people involved in the movement. There is great value for people who are involved in the greening of faith to participate in this global community of practice called the Transition Movement. A sustainable human presence on planet Earth requires healthy communities that have cohesion and resilience at local and regional levels—and Transition helps them work at the grassroots to build those kinds of communities.[62]

Rani, Transition Palo Alto, California

Prerana Jayakumar, who goes by the name of Rani, is Hindu and a member of Transition Palo Alto, California. Rani is a stay-at-home mother of two, teaches Indian classical music, and is passionate about sharing and crafting. She reflects that joy in her participation with Transition.

Rani Jayakumar with her husband Narayan Sundarajan,
son Smaran Narayanan (age 7), and daughter Dhyana Narayanan (age 4)
(*photo by Rani's father, Raghavan Jayakumar*)

"I think my faith and Transition were always interconnected, even before I knew Transition existed. I feel like I had always seen, from my childhood visits and life in India, the vision of a positive future that could mean happiness through being with loved ones, just talking and singing and dancing and playing, not by having a lot of toys or watching TV, but by eating together, telling stories and jokes, and engaging in religious traditions. Here in the United States environmentalism can often be gloomy, with a dim view of the future, but in India social interaction is an essential component of a happy life.

"In the south of India, the festival of Navarathri, involves going from house to house to sing songs in praise of goddesses. The hosts display their family gods and various beautiful dolls and scenes up on steps for visitors to see. Each piece has a story of how it came into the household. The visitors sing and then eat warm lentils full of protein for the winter months. I remember going with my cousins and neighbors, all dressed up in traditional silks, to sing in our little voices, and eat at every single house until our bellies were bursting. This is just one example of how religious festivals and day-to-day events are linked with the community and the seasons. This is what Transition is about for me—stories, traditional skills and arts, living with the seasons, community. I saw [the documentary] *In Transition 1.0* and it spoke to all those things—I was hooked.

"I was always taught that Hinduism is not a religion — it's a way of life. In India, it informs every aspect of the Hindu's culture — clothing, the red bindi on the forehead, cooking, visits to temples, marriage, family life, and rituals. A fundamental part of that culture is to take only what you need, to use every resource to its fullest, and to make use of materials that are available. For example, the banana tree is very important to Indians and Hindus in particular. The leaves are used as plates or fans or wrappers for food, whole trees make entrances and announce weddings, the stringy thread that comes off of the tree makes string and rope for tying and stringing flowers, bananas are used in every offering to gods as well as people, and everything from flowers to plantains to the tree trunk itself can be cooked and eaten. The remainder is given to animals or composted in piles. This holistic view holds that we consider the Earth itself (the goddess Bhoodevi) and all living things are sacred. It informs the idea of using what you have to make a self-sufficient system, which is what Transition is all about.

"India is a place where people are very interconnected. There is not much privacy, but in exchange, you get community. Neighbors share food and tools and goods, hand-me-downs come from cousins and neighbors, and every religious festival is an excuse to gather with friends and family. This is a huge part of Transition for me — sharing with neighbors, living in a gift economy, sharing not just stuff but stories, history, and experiences.

"I'm energized by the positive vision of the future Transition has given me. Transition has helped me appreciate what I already have in my culture. It has helped me see the value in the rituals and traditions I used to dismiss as tedious, superstitious, or simply backward. I take pride now in learning to make flower garlands, adorning hands with henna, or memorizing a long traditional scripture in praise of the rainy season. As a teacher of classical Hindu music, I have tried to instill in my students and their families the value of our resources and our culture, to show them that what their parents and grandparents knew is still relevant and more important now than ever."

Hindu Declaration on Climate Change

People of faith around the globe are reaching deep into their traditions to find how their faith can guide them in these uncertain times. Here is an excerpt from the Hindu Declaration on Climate Change:

"[W]e call on all Hindus to expand our conception of dharma. We must consider the effects of our actions not just on ourselves and those humans around us, but also on all beings. We have a dharmic duty for each of us to do our part in ensuring that we have a functioning, abundant, and bountiful planet."[63]

Sikh Statement on Climate Change

The Sikh Statement on Climate Change was presented by *EcoSikh* on September 18, 2014:

> "You, Yourself created the Universe, and You are pleased...You, Yourself the bumblebee, flower, fruit and the tree. You, Yourself the water, desert, ocean and the pond. You, Yourself are the big fish, tortoise and the Cause of causes." —Guru Granth Sahib, Maru Sohele, 1020

> "Through His teachings, our first guru, Guru Nanak Dev Ji, explained that the world we humans create around ourselves is a reflection of our own inner state. So as we look around to our wasteful and polluting practices, we obtain an insight into the chaos within us... Respect for nature is ingrained in Sikh teachings. As Guru Nanak Ji said: 'Pawan Guru pani pita mata dharat mahat (Air is our teacher, water our father and the great sacred earth is our mother). If we act now, we can protect our atmosphere, water resources and earth for ourselves and for future generations. To achieve internal peace, we must first look at the environment in which we live.'"[64]

Islam and the Environment

The following statement is from a gathering in Dubai in 2013 titled, "Islam and the Environment: Global Summit for Sustainable Living."

> "Islam's message is strong and clear when it comes to preserving the environment and respecting nature: these are the inherent values of the faith. With the world's attention shifting towards climate change and the role in the rapid destruction of our environment, ethical principles promoted by Islam that encourage green living need to be acknowledged and promoted.

> "The environment lies at the core of the Islamic faith, and the underlying principle that forms the foundation of the Prophet Mohammed's (PBUH) holistic environmental vision is the belief in the interdependency between all natural elements, and the premise that if humans abuse or exhaust one element, the natural world as a whole will suffer direct consequences. The Qur'an clearly explains that humankind holds a privileged position among God's creations on Earth: he or she is chosen as khalifa, 'vice-regent' and is entrusted with an *amana*—the responsibility of caring for God's earthly creations."[65]

Stories play an important role in all faith traditions. Some are ancient stories that guide us today and some are the stories of people living out their faith in this time of uncertainty. Often these are stories of hope that help us believe in the goodness that exists in the universe.

Phil Metzler: Transition Boulder, Colorado, and Transition Goshen, Indiana

Phil Metzler, a Mennonite and member of both Transition Boulder, Colorado, where he grew up, and Transition Goshen, Indiana, where he went to college. He shared that his faith provides a good foundation for being open to Transition and permaculture as a worldview.

"Some of the values of simplicity in the Mennonite tradition focus on social justice with an emphasis on service, practical gifting of one's resources and abilities to one's community and further abroad, and in thinking about our relationships with others. The well-known statements, 'Think globally, act locally' and 'Live simply so others can simply live,' were things that I grew up with in my community, so they shaped my openness to making a difference wherever I lived.

"Being somewhat marginalized as a person of faith in Boulder, Colorado, predisposed me to be part of a movement that is somewhat different. My grandfather was Amish, so that was part of what I was exposed to. My formal education was engineering, which was very secular. All my education was secular. The counterpoint to that was my work in Chile, where my wife's family lived.

"I draw on my faith background to see the difference between a dominant worldview and my faith worldview. I was fortunate to be exposed to permaculture to see how that can change the worldview, so I looked to find a different path."

Transition Goshen members at a workshop planning a permaculture garden.
(*photo by Phil Metzler*)

For Phil what has been interesting is the sense of a common good. It has become more evident in the move to Goshen from Boulder. His enthusiasm for the move was to ask what would Transition look like in a different kind of community where the community was predominantly faith-centered. The Chamber of Commerce in Goshen actually branded the city around the theme of "common good." The agricultural framework is still very much a small-farm orientation. Goshen College is Mennonite and there are many Amish.

"I was active with the permaculture community when Transition emerged. I saw that Transition was the path for which I had been searching to use the permaculture principles for community work. In Boulder, faith communities are marginalized; you have to tread softly if talking about faith when working in the community. I treaded carefully when first participating in Transition Town Boulder. I recognized that my faith community had a lot to bring to the community work—especially the ideas of Inner Transition. I was only able to bring the ideas from my faith community into the work, but not specifically, or as a tangible or significant outward contribution. It made the Inner Transition work meaningful and maybe it sucked me into the Transition.

"I was a big fan of David Holmgren and his work on future scenarios (*Future Scenarios: How Communities Can Adapt to Peak Oil and Climate Change*). I thought it was great to think in longer time frames—to think of hope and faith as active terms. One of the darker aspects of these converging crises is that there wasn't the inclination to hold them at arms length or avoid them, but still address them. In the church as a whole, you're always working against insurmountable odds, like beloved community or grand reform. That's faith. In Transition we accept that things are going to happen, the best we can do is to build community and capacity. It's very complimentary to our faith.

"The church doesn't want to dwell on the depressing issues of the day. How can I bring the joy of working in Transition to the congregation? Stewardship and Creation Care are rich, but how do we learn to recognize our interdependence, to flip some of the hierarchy of 'man over nature' on end and get out of the disconnect we're in? Transition has challenged my faith and focused it. Instead of being in a faith community, just to be part of it, it has given me new questions.

"If there's one overarching thing, it's the narrative, the story, as a whole. It really gives people the opportunity to think about being a people of a longer period of time. How do we fit our actions into that story and bring our worldview into something much broader? Transition is trying to bring the conversation about the narrative or story into the community. What are the gifts that Transition brings? What are the stories?—Not just heady philosophical or theological stuff, but that which brings it down to real work.

"I have been inspired by the work of David Korten, author of *When Corporations Rule the World*. Many people in the Transition movement believe that Korten's books resonate with the movement's goal to strengthen local communities, versus supporting multinational corporations."

Carolyn Baker, Transition Boulder, Colorado

Many people involved in Transition may not be involved in a faith community, but consider themselves spiritual. Carolyn Baker is the author of several works since 2007 that have focused on emotional and spiritual preparation for an uncertain future. She was part of Transition Boulder, Colorado, during its existence.

"I am not a person of faith, but my spiritual path has led me to write, speak, and teach about how to prepare emotionally and spiritually for living in a post-industrial world and a world profoundly altered by catastrophic climate change. If we are not able to make meaning of our predicament, and if we do not have a sense of what we came here to do and the gifts we can offer each other and the planet, then we are destined to be overcome with despair, cynicism, and possibly not wanting to be here at all. My perspective on these issues is laid out very clearly in my book.[66]

"Spirituality has informed my work with Transition and other groups by motivating me to look deeply inside myself and ask the question: Who do I want to be during this time of Transition? And who, after all, is asking the question? What gifts do I have to offer all living beings? How can I cultivate qualities such as compassion, community building, skillful communication, and emotional literacy in order to serve the human and non-human community? Poetry, art, music, and deep ecology have significantly informed my work in the world."

Her questions and concerns are not dissimilar to those of the people we've already heard from. There doesn't seem to be a large chasm between people of faith and those without faith communities who see themselves as spiritual.

Starhawk

We who do belong to faith communities come from a myriad of traditions. Some consider themselves "pagans." A prominent neopagan community today is the Reclaiming Community, which was inspired by the writings and actions of a woman named Starhawk. Starhawk is a permaculture instructor and has connected the permaculture principles to social activism. She is also a strong supporter of the Transition Movement. The following is a statement about the belief in deep connection with Earth from the Reclaiming Community's "Reclaiming Principles of Unity." It resonates with what we've learned throughout this chapter.

"The values of the Reclaiming tradition stem from our understanding that the earth is alive and all of life is sacred and interconnected. We see the Goddess as immanent in the earth's cycles of birth, growth, death, decay and regeneration. Our practice arises from a deep, spiritual commitment to the earth, to healing, and to the linking of magic with political action.... Our tradition honors the wild, and calls for service to the earth and the community.... All living beings are worthy of respect. All are supported by the sacred elements of air, fire, water and earth. We work to create and sustain communities and cultures that embody our values that can help to heal the wounds of the earth and her peoples, and that can sustain us and nurture future generations."[67]

How inspiring these people are! It is so beautiful to see the similarities within the differences shared by these "Transitioners." We have learned how our faith can be brought into the Transition work, even without naming it. We have seen how the movement can shape our relationship with our faith community. And we see the joy that each person has experienced as a part of their work in Transition. Even though faith is not part of the discussion in Transition Town, it very much guides us. Since its inception there has been a steady increase in numbers of participants, Initiatives, and countries involved. What is the root of that success? And in what ways does faith and Transition intersect?

Although a faith community could form a Transition community, most likely that is not practical or possible. Today most people travel far to their places of worship. They come from different communities where the demographics could be very different. There could be a mix of people from rural, suburban, and urban areas. Some communities could be industrial and others agricultural. If the purpose of Transition is to strengthen community ties and build resilience, faith communities can play a supporting and validating role. They could open their facilities to meetings of a local Transition community. They could host Transition Trainings, as well as celebrations and regular Transition meetings. People who are members of that faith community who live nearby could join the Transition Initiative and report about the progress of that Initiative. Members could make sure that their faith community is a "good neighbor" that encourages the work of the Initiative.

Sebastopol's Village Building Convergence
(*photo by David Ferrera*)

CHAPTER 6
RISING TO THE CHALLENGE
WITH INNOVATION, CREATIVITY, AND LOVE

Sing and rejoice, ye children of the day and of the light; for the Lord is at work in this thick night of darkness that may be felt. And truth doth flourish as the rose, and the lilies do grow among the thorns, and the plants atop the hills, and upon them the lambs do skip and play. And never heed the tempests nor the storms, floods nor rains, for the seed Christ is over all, and doth reign. And so be of good faith and valiant for the truth: for the truth can live in the jails. And fear not the loss of the fleece, for it will grow again; and follow the lamb, if it be under the beast's horns, or under the beast's heels; for the lamb shall have the victory over them all.

— George Fox[68]

"Because everyone is welcome to the table; because it's egalitarian; because I care about the fate of the planet and know I can't do it alone; because of the focus on the Inner Transition; because it's fun." These are some of the most common responses when people are asked what drew them to be part of a Transition Initiative. And many of the same answers come from people of faith who are drawn to Transition. The common thread seems to be the Transition Movement's emphasis on love — people care, earth care, fair share. Like many faith communities, Transition is about healthy relationships — making others feel welcome by listening, sharing, and connecting with what is within.

Further, healthy communities flourish with innovation, creativity, flexibility and helping people to love themselves. They become stagnant when change is avoided, when routine is mandated. Faith communities have to rise to other challenges — the emergence of different worldviews or pressures from social and political movements. Many have changed with the times without losing their core belief systems or succumbing to apathy. They've been innovative in working with young people to keep them involved.

97

"Because what we're fighting for now is each other. We have to fight for the person sitting next to us and the person living next door to us, for the person across town and across the tracks from us, and for the person across the continent and across the ocean from us. Because we're fighting for our humanity. That's what solidarity is. That's what love looks like."   — Tim DeChristopher [69]

"And if our past social movements are any indication, we know that there will be points where there is no reasonable expectation that we will win this struggle. And in those dark moments, we will have to continue the struggle for justice, not because we expect that things will be OK. In those dark moments, we will continue the struggle for climate justice because that's what it means to be faithful to a God who loves this world. We will continue this struggle because that is what it means to be faithful to the people and to the world that we love. — Wen Stephenson[70]

The challenge is for communities to stay cohesive and relevant in an age of cynicism and fragmentation induced by the Internet and other aspects of "globalization." Many people today have come to assume that all the answers to life can be found on the World Wide Web. So why continue with what seems to be antiquated ideas and practices? A faith group and a Transition Initiative both attract people by speaking to their needs and by evolving as new needs and challenges have emerged. What began in a small town in England has had to rise to the challenge of quick expansion into a huge variety of social, political, and geographical settings.

Growth of the Movement

Innovation and creativity has kept the Transition Movement alive. What began as an experiment in a market town in England has expanded across the continent in an amazing configuration of settings. When Rob was first asked to help form a Transition Initiative in another town, he replied, "You have to figure this out for yourself." But not long after that encounter he and others realized that people needed some sort of blueprint. From that understanding emerged the first book, *The Transition Handbook*.

When people got hold of that book, they thought it had the answers. They hoped if they followed the step-by-step instructions that they could replicate the Totnes experience. But soon they found that their towns were different, that their cities were too big, or that their villages lacked enterprise. *The Transition Handbook* was meant as a guide, not as a bible for success. The founders realized that what was needed was a hands-on workshop to help people tap into their own creativity and to help them see how there was no one right way to work towards resilience. Those weekend workshops were so successful, that along with the book, sprinkles of Transition Towns grew in England, then across Europe, and then without bounds.

Although not prescriptive, there are some principles to guide participants. They are:

1) positive visioning,

2) helping people access good information and trust them to make good decisions,

3) inclusion and openness,

4) building resilience,

5) inner and outer Transition,

6) subsidiarity: self-organization and decision making at the appropriate level, and

7) power with.

With all the success bubbling in towns across England and spreading into Europe there was a new challenge facing the Movement. Would they be able to rise to that challenge? How would the residents of Paris, or Barcelona, or São Paulo, or Los Angeles bring millions of people to the table? How could they possibly be a Transition "Town?" How could they all fit into a room to map out a course towards resilience? It couldn't be found in the handbook or in the workshops.

But because people were encouraged to be creative and imaginative, a solution was found. The "hub" movement began. Large cities can be broken down into districts or barrios, and there people could come together to share their concerns and their hopes and dreams for a better, more resilient place to live. Each of those sections of the city sent representatives to the "hub" where the pieces of the quilt of the city could be seen as a whole. This approach was used in Barcelona, Paris, and Los Angeles. Was it easy? No way. But it was a way to bring to life the ideals of the Transition Movement in large geographic and population areas. It was a way to assure that the community-building, innovative thinking, and creative actions would include people no matter where they lived.

The Transition Network still saw the challenges of bringing people together in large districts of cities, where possibly there were still tens of thousands of residents. And, like magic, the concept of

Transition Neighborhoods emerged. But not really magic — it took a number of people who knew that the movement could not be limited by space or by numbers of people. It took the creative and imaginative and fluid thinking and hours of discussion and experimentation to meet the challenge. Why not define the space where a Transition Initiative could grow and thrive as any space? And then when some neighborhoods were too big to gather people together easily, Transition Streets were born.

Transition Streets is the latest innovation to come from the Transition Network to rise to the challenge that every place on Earth is different and needs a different approach to birthing an Initiative! It's exciting, creative, and practical.

> "Transition Streets brings neighbors together to learn how to save energy, water, and money; reduce waste; and build social cohesion that will help neighbors 'weather the storm' in times of emergency. Transition Streets is taking root in dozens of neighborhoods across the US — from Bozeman, Montana, to Charlottesville, Virginia."[71]

An example of what good can come from a Transition Street Initiative comes from San Diego, California. California has experienced a severe drought over the last several years, threatening food supplies to the whole nation. In mid-city San Diego a number of neighbors concerned about water conservation came together to see what they could do. Jamie Edmonds, a resident, gathered together his neighbors to see what they could do to encourage conservation. They used the Transition Streets workbook on saving water and energy. From that they learned how to measure their water usage and take steps, either with an investment, or cost-free, to reduce their use of water. Many of the neighbors had not known one another before this. Now they meet regularly to explore conservation ideas. KPBS reported:

> "Organizers say the program can save homeowners up to $900 a year and cut their carbon emissions by 1.3 tons. But Edmonds said there's another, equally important outcome, 'Yeah you save a bunch of money, yeah you reduce your carbon footprint, but you also create a support community that is invaluable. I don't see how you put a price on that.'"[72]

There is continuing creativity of people when they are given a chance to share ideas and get to know their neighbors. But how is it possible for people to feel a part of a larger movement? Isn't there the possibility that people will still feel alone in their efforts to transition to a fossil-fuel-free society or to stem the tide of climate change, climate chaos, and economic instability? The Transition Network and Transition US teams work hard to engage people across the planet, inviting them to share their experiences and hosting conferences. But sometimes an individual or small group of people create a new type of connection with others in the Movement.

Pamela Boyce Simms, Transition Trainer

Pamela Boyce Simms, a certified Transition Trainer with Transition US, helped found and is Convener of the Mid-Atlantic Transition Hub (MATH). She saw the possibility that connecting Transition Initiatives from an area that has a lot in common, though widely dispersed, might strengthen and maintain those Initiatives.

Pamels Boyce Simms
(*photo by Jim Peppler*)

Pamela is a Buddhist and a Quaker. She shared an intriguing story about how her Buddhist practice led her to Transition. It was during a four-year retreat in the Karma Triyana Dharmachakra Monastery in Woodstock, New York. The head of the Karma Kagyu school of Tibetan Buddhism, the Seventeenth Gyalwang karmapa, Ogyen Trinley Dorje, handed out a mandate to all monasteries to find an environmental movement near to where their monastery was located. Pamela began asking around the area of Woodstock and someone suggested she attend a Transition Training that was happening nearby. Although, "the training didn't take," she said she was intrigued by some of the teachings in the handouts and by the theories. She read some of Rob Hopkins's work and after learning he was a Buddhist realized he was a kindred spirit. He had imbedded his understanding of systems theory from permaculture into the Transition Movement, something that resonated with her. Pamela soon started a Transition Town in Woodstock.

"It wasn't really my idea to start MATH. It was the people on the ground, those involved in or trying to involve others in Transition where the Movement wasn't flourishing. The Transitioners in the Mid-Atlantic Corridor had a challenge, due to the preponderance of urban, suburban, exurban, areas. 'Exurban' describes the ring of prosperous communities beyond the suburbs that are commuter towns for an urban area. Many people in these areas are strongly oriented to the corporate capitalism culture, which doesn't predispose them to be part of an egalitarian, non-hierarchical, local environmental movement. At the same time there are a number of rural areas as well, adding more challenges to finding common ground.

"Because people in the Mid-Atlantic did not easily take to the kind of grass-roots movement that has so enamored Great Britain, a different approach is needed to help the Transition Movement penetrate into the area. So MATH has a council with 21 representatives from six states. Each representative is a contact back to people in their states. Some of those people are in Transition Initiatives, are Transitioners, or are wanting to connect with Transition. They are 'holding the pilot lights' in their states. The Movement may not be flourishing yet, but those pilot lights won't let it die. They know they are out there as the outpost for Transition, and what they have gained so far grounds them. They are not necessarily growing a population of Transitioners, but they are growing the Movement in a different way from what other organizations are doing.

The MATH Council meets in cyber space monthly and face-to-face twice a year, usually in a central location in New Jersey. They share practices, challenges, and successes, and talk about burnout, and other experiences.

"The movement really needs people who are living the life that Transition espouses. People need to walk the talk. So a new council has been formed, a Spokescouncil, that is joining together Quakers, eco-Buddhists, and other faith representatives from across the country who are more willing to challenge themselves to walk that talk. They are meeting in cyberspace to support and nourish one another through conversation and contact. I have a special interest in helping create and maintain an egalitarian network.

"Cultivating a leaderful, egalitarian movement is fundamental to the Transition conversation in the Mid-Atlantic region, from New York to Virginia. A Spokescouncil of Egalitarian Resilience Networks has emerged within the Mid-Atlantic Transition Hub constellation. The Spokescouncil is intended to hold the MATH network accountable to the Transition movement's egalitarian, social permaculture roots.

"Networks that form part of our operational core are invited to be part of the Spokescouncil. Those networks: 1) vigilantly listen for and address the emergent need of the whole while honoring innate

Fixers Adam Lota and Dustin Buccino working on a weed wacker,
Transition Pasadena, California's Repair Café
(*Photo by Maelane Chan*)

gifts of individuals, and 2) value and seek continual system transformation and refinement in service to the whole. The Spokescouncil's primary goal is to continually support and challenge participants to deepen egalitarian, whole systems thinking and practices within their networks even as we foster social transformation through our work."

Innovation and creativity is the name of the game! Incredible ideas have emerged across the globe. Sometimes it's so simple, as in the case of Transition Town Charlotte, Vermont's desire to transform some lawn at the library into an edible food garden. Or sometimes it's complex, as in Transition Brixton, England, which has created a local currency.

Transition Pasadena, California's Repair Café brings together "fixers" and community members to repair used and broken items. The project has saved more than 1800 items—from toasters to vacuums—from going to the landfill, but the greatest impact is the sense of community being built along the way. "Payment" for a repair job was that the person receiving the service had to sit down and share and story from their life. The Repair Café was featured in the Los Angeles Times and in Rob Hopkins's newest book, *21 Stories of Transition*.[73]

Collaboration in the Transition Movement

Most people involved with Transition do not think they can or need to act on their own. The Initiatives most often collaborate with other organizations and efforts already existing in their community. Steve Chase and I created the "Quakers in Transition" website to reach out to all Quakers because Quaker beliefs intersect so well with the Movement that we thought that other Quakers might be interested in finding or founding a Transition Initiative near them.

> "Quakers In Transition is an online project of the New England Yearly Meeting Earthcare Ministry Committee. Our goal is to support Friends working in the Transition Movement. Gathering strength from our faith tradition, we seek to work with our neighbors and address the challenges of peak oil, climate change, and a dysfunctional global economy with courage, creativity, and a positive vision for our communities."[74]

Most of us know the path of organizing in a community. Often there comes a time when interests wane and the group seems at a bit of a loss for new direction. Good things have happened, but maybe it's at a standstill. Well, again the good thinking and innovation of Transition folks has created a new workshop, Thrive. This workshop focuses, not on the ideals of the movement, but on how to sustain the life of the Initiative. But can one group of people bring about the changes necessary for a post-oil world? What can a small group accomplish? The key to that dilemma is "collaboration."

Transition Town Charlotte (TTC) works with the town Energy Committee, the Conservation Commission, the library, the Grange, the Congregational Church, the school, 350VT, and any other group that has an idea and wants to join forces. Our community gardens; annual electronic waste collection; appearances at board meetings to support group efforts; presentations of speakers, workshops, or documentaries; and local-foods potlucks wouldn't be successful without the collaboration of others.

TTC has supported a group that is working to stop construction of a natural gas pipeline proposed to run through the northern part of our state. We have signed on to letters and statements opposed to the fossil fuel infrastructure. Many from our group have been present at local and national demonstrations related to creating a fossil fuel-free world. We have supported and encouraged renewable energy projects.

On a larger scale, Transition Towns are working with organizations such as trade unions, conservation trusts, housing trusts, farmers, and a host of environmental and religious organizations. We have a history of collaborating with 350.org nationally and locally, with state Interfaith Power & Light organizations, Slow Food, and other national movements and organizations.

We are rising to the challenge together. We assess where the need is and adapt to changes as needed to stay vital and meaningful in our communities.

This iterative process of study, social experiment, observation, and reflection is ongoing and is perhaps even becoming a stronger norm within the Transition Movement. For example, Rob Hopkins argued that Transition organizers should always challenge themselves to avoid any situation where their understanding and application of the Transition analysis, vision, and strategy "becomes ossified and encourages slavish adherence rather than creativity and innovation." To shake things up further, Rob put forth the principle that the Transition Movement should be "continually learning from its successes and its failures and redefining itself, trying to research what is working and what isn't."

> "Transition has evolved and grown hugely since the first *Transition Handbook*. The principle of it being an iterative process, of the sharing of failures being as important as the successes, has done it a great service, and much has been learned as a result. New models and tools have been developed, and as a result the second edition of the *Handbook* will look very different from the first, but it will also, I hope, actually be a more familiar representation of the Transition you know, and also a more useful tool." [75]

But how does a small group of people who come together for potlucks, fun, sharing, and education have any kind of influence in the place where they live? The Transition Movement stresses that an Initiative cannot be some kind of exclusive group—gathering and educating in isolation of the government structure, or of other organizations within the town or city. Making connections is an essential part of a successful Transition Initiative. But how do we really invite racially and culturally diverse people to participate? White Privilege conferences and other mechanisms are available to those who are committed to learning what steps are needed to be more inclusive.

Energy-descent planning and gaining the support of the local government is a key feature of the Transition Movement's local organizing model, but it is now envisioned as the product of sustained community involvement and input and typically happens late in the local Transition organizing process. Workshops that focus on creating relationships with town governments are helpful. In one such workshop we received many tips about approaching town or city political leaders, and we participated in role-plays to prepare us for this next step. Although opportunities for innovation don't present themselves regularly in a small town like Charlotte, Vermont, we do have good working relationships and recognition within the town.

It is widely recognized that all the possible renewable energy projects in the future will not fully replace what fossil fuels have provided. So we need to begin to plan for what a community looks like if there's less energy available. We in the Northeast United States are very used to weather-related power outages that last from a day to as long as a week. We learn to adapt to less energy by massive conservation efforts. For some it becomes a fun challenge. Our lives slow down. We get outside more. We visit with our neighbors and have candlelight potlucks. While power outages carry the danger of not having enough heat or of losing food in the freezers, they do provide an opportunity to experience life that can be rich and full with less consumption.

An Energy Descent Plan helps put into place suggestions for conserving energy and preparing alternatives in our homes such as backup wood heat or an outdoor area to store frozen food. Ice houses were common many years ago. We have talked about experimenting with one, since there is a pond nearby where we could cut blocks of ice to supply an ice house. But that's an extreme step we may not need. Canning and root cellars don't need electricity. Solar panels with battery backup can provide needed energy when the grid is down. The Energy Descent Plan should prepare the whole community for the eventuality of less fossil fuel power. It can be an exciting, collaborative, and creative process for everyone.

Such forward thinking is how and why the Transition Movement has flourished and grown. This is why there is still excitement after 10 years. And many important and caring people are aware of and talking about the Movement, including Naomi Klein, author of the challenging and very important book, *This Changes Everything: Capitalism vs. the Climate.*

"A lot of what we call apathy is just people not knowing how to deal with the overwhelming emotions. So you just push it away. The way in which our movements are now structured, particularly environmental movements, but many movements, is these NGOs — we communicate—it used to be with mailings, now it's Tweets and emails—and it ends up being a lot of fear-based messaging, but then nothing about what to do with that fear. Scare you—click on this. The idea is you're going to be scared so you'll become an activist. But that's not actually how humans behave. You get scared and you want to curl up in a ball right? So we need spaces to grieve, and to actually talk about how frightening this is... the Transition Town movement has this part of it that they call 'Inner Transition,' which is addressing this reality. That it isn't just an outer transition, but also we have to go through our own personal transformation, and that also involves expressing that grief. It's something that the feminist movement has done well, and a lot of people in the Transition Town movement who are part of this Inner Transition piece of it, come out of the feminist movement, because there's an understanding that when you   collapse peoples' worldviews, you have to stick around to pick up the pieces."[76]

We're here to pick up the pieces. We support each other. We have fun together. We do things that don't cost money; instead they just take time, and an effort to be fully present in our community. We can rise to the challenge of our times, together in faith, in hope, and with love.

Looking Ahead

We know we need a story that holds a "radical dreaming" and touches the hearts of people, and that climate change is a symptom of a cause that corporate media cannot admit. Industrial civilisation has brought the living systems on which we depend to a breaking point—systems that do not operate according to our 21st technology, 18th century reason, nor our 4000 BC sense of godlike control.... The obvious "solution" to power-down our whole way of life was never on the table. At the COP21 "fringe" however it's clear we need to do exactly that.... The first thing you notice is that everything connects. The second, that there is no hostility.

—Charlotte Du Cann[77]

As this book goes to print in early 2016, the COP21 talks in Paris are behind us. Although an accord was signed, the conclusion from many observers is that it's not enough. Bill McKibben wrote:

"So the world emerges, finally, with something like a climate accord, albeit unenforceable. If all parties kept their promises, the planet would warm by an estimated 6.3 degrees Fahrenheit, or 3.5 degrees Celsius, above preindustrial levels. And that is way, way too much. We are set to pass the 1 degree Celsius mark this year, and that's already enough to melt ice caps and push the sea level threateningly higher.

"The irony is, an agreement like this adopted at the first climate conference in 1995 might have worked. Even then it wouldn't have completely stopped global warming, but it would have given us a chance of meeting the 1.5 degree-Celsius target that the world notionally agreed on."[78]

Lindsey Cook, the Quaker United Nations Office representative in Bonn, Germany, was involved with quiet diplomacy among the COP 21 negotiators and had this to share:

"But something is missing from the negotiations, even from Al Gore's uplifting talks on renewable energies ('enough energy arrives from the sun in one hour to meet the power needs of the entire world for a full year!'). It is the narrative on living sustainably, on questioning the assumption of unlimited material growth on a planet with limited natural resources. Many negotiators would argue that lifestyle choice or regulation are national initiatives and not relevant in an international treaty. But when this narrative is sidelined, the potential to see the solution to climate change as a technical fix is intensified."[79]

Supplying that missing element is the call for the Transition Movement! We are here to work at the grassroots level, hoping to change ourselves, and our communities, and hopefully have an effect on the world.

How can we be hopeful when we see the rise of mass shootings in my country? When there continues the trend of unjust actions and killing of unarmed black men by increasingly militarized police? When anti-Muslim rhetoric is increasing? When the sea levels continue to rise and the planet continues to unravel with no end in sight?

Where We Can Find Hope

Finding rays of hope in the midst of all of this is the work of Transition Towns. We must rise to the challenge of increasing racism and inequality, for the issues of climate change and injustice are inextricably connected.

Greenfaith: Interfaith Partners for the Environment is an excellent source for learning about the foundations for Earthcare from many faiths.[80]

"When God created the first human beings, God led them around the Garden of Eden and said: 'Look at my works! See how beautiful they are—how excellent! For your sake I created them all. See to it that you do not spoil and destroy My world; for if you do, there will be no one else to repair it.'"[81]

In the Jewish liturgy there is a prayer called "Aleinu" in which we ask that the world be soon perfected under the sovereignty of God (*le-takein 'olam be-malkhut Shaddai*). *Tikkun 'olam*, the perfecting or the repairing of the world, has become a major theme in modern Jewish social justice theology.[82] It is usually expressed as an activity, which must be done by humans in partnership with God. It is an important concept in light of the tasks ahead of us. In our ignorance and our greed, we have damaged the world and silenced many of the voices of the choir of Creation. Now we must fix it. There is no one else to repair it but us.

We can find hope in the work of so many people of faith who are finding sources of inspiration to make a better world from their sacred texts and common ground to stand up against the injustices, many of which are caused by our destruction of the planet.

We can find hope in all those people of faith rising to the challenge and making the connections between their beliefs and care for Earth.

We can find hope in those whose wisdom is active in the change.

We can find hope in the work of millions of people around the globe who are working diligently to turn the tide of global warming, and are working for justice and equality.

We can find hope when we work with our neighbors, active in our Transition Initiatives.

We can find hope in the wisdom of Carolyn Treadway, who said she became committed to Transition when she read this quote from Rob Hopkins because it was a description of the kind of life she wanted to live:

> "The Energy Descent Plan should be more like a holiday greeting and when you read it you should feel bereft if you do not spend the rest of your life working on this."[83]

She took a weekend Transition Training and made a commitment to bring the news of Transition home to Bloomington-Normal, Illinois.

We can find hope in other organizations embracing the idea of resilience. The Post Carbon Institute recently published a document, "Six Foundations for Building Community Resilience," and one of the reviewers was from Transition US. We attended a "Jobs, Justice, and Climate" rally in Boston, where we heard from a variety of indigenous people, union organizers, religious leaders, and justice and climate organizers. When people from different callings recognize that their work is the same work, they will rise with strength and conviction and be heard.

We can find hope in this uplifting piece from Transition US:

You Know You're in Transition When...

1) *You know your neighbors.*

2) *You know what "400 ppm" means.*

3) *You believe everything can be recycled.*

4) *You have an unusual appreciation for chickens.*

5) *You know which foods are in season.*

6) *You think work parties are fun.*

7) *You are aware that our global bee populations, fish stocks, and climate stability are all in serious danger and are all related.*

8) *You're passionate about composting, clotheslines, or graywater (... probably all three).*

9) *Your favorite mode of entertainment is a re-skilling fair.*

10) *You dream of local-scale solar power stations, community currencies, public gardens or tool-sharing libraries.*

11) *You know that the "radical" notion of a post-growth economy is simply common sense.*

12) *You see that happiness is not about how much "stuff" you have, but about meaningful connections to your community and to nature.*

But most of all... You know what a better world looks like, and are grateful to play a part in bringing it to life.[84]

We can find hope in being part of a Transition Initiative that brings people together who can support and encourage each other. It becomes an extended family, a family with a purpose, a family who care about the community where they live, a family who have a common vision of a resilient community that can rise to the challenge of climate chaos, diminishing fossil fuels, and economic uncertainty.

We can find hope in the faith has guides us onto many paths that intersect in care for people and the planet. It guides us to want to make a difference in our communities, our states, our countries, and our world. And because of our communities of faith, we are supported in that work. Without the label of "faith," the Transition Movement is a faithful community of people, respecting one another and Earth, looking for a transition from a fossil-fuel-based consumer society, to one that cares deeply for healthy relationships, walks gently on the earth, and rises to action on behalf of all that lives.

Together we will rise to the challenge!

Endnotes

Full references are found in the *Bibliography* following.

1 Reverend Peter Sawtell blogs at <eco-justice.org>.

2 Rabbi Arthur Waskow blogs at <theshalomcenter.org/blog>.

3 Starhawk blogs at <starhawksblog.org>.

4 The *QIF Focus Books* are availabe at Quakerbooks.org, Amazon.com, and other online bookstores. They are also available for download at <quakerin-stitute.org> with suggested donation.

5 Mahasiddha Machig Lhadbron <chodpaorg.wordpress.com/machik-labdron-2>.

6 Rob Hopkins blogs at *Transition Culture* <transitionnetwork.org/blogs/rob-hopkins>.

7 Ruah Swennerfelt blogs at <transitionvision.org>.

8 Elizabeth G. Watson, *Healing Ourselves and the Earth*, Quaker Earthcare Witness <quakerearthcare.org/publications>.

9 Erik Andrus, *The Burlington Free Press* <burlingtonfreepress.com>.

10 Paul Hawken, 2008.

11 Transition Network <transitionnetwork.org>.

12 Pope Francis' Encyclical <w2.vatican.va/content/dam/francesco/pdf/encyc-licals/documents/papa-francesco_20150524_enciclica-laudato-si _en.pdf>.

13 Rabbi Rachel Barenblat <reformjudaism.org/blog/blog-author/rabbi-rachel-barenblat>

14 Starhawk, 1993.

15 Hazrat Inayat Khan <hazratinayatkhan.org>.

16 Robert Van der Weyer, 2003.

17 Rabbi Andrea Cohen-Kiener, 2009.

18 Paul Hawken, 2008.

19 Martin Luther King, Jr. "Remaining Awake Through a Great Revolution." Speech delivered at the National Cathedral, Washington, D.C., 31 March 1968.

20 Friends World Committee for Consultation, 2012. *Kabarak Call to Peace and Eco-Justice* <fwcc.world/call.pdf>.

21 Rogat Mshana, World Council of Churches <oikoumene.org>.

22 North American Conference of the World Council of Churches, *There's a New World in the Making* <oikoumene.org/en/member-churches/north-america>.

23 *Matthew* 6:33 (King James version)

24 Paul Anderson, 2013.

25 Ayse Kadayifc essay in Waskow and Berman, 2011.

26 Marty Ostrow and Terry Kay Rockefeller, *Renewal* <renewalproject.net/film/story/credits>.

27 Mark Wallace, 2010.

28 Green Sangha <greensangha.org>.

29 Interfaith Power & Light History <interfaithpowerandlight.org/about/mission-history>.

30 Dorothy Day quoted in Nancy L. Brooks, 1984, p. 109.

31 Rob Hopkins, 2015

32 David Holmgren, 2002

33 Rob Hopkins, 2006. *Permaculture Magazine* <resilience.org/stories/2006-11-02/powerdown-and-permaculture-cusp-transition>.

34 Bob Edwards, 1995. "With Liberty and Environmental Justice for All: The Emergence and Challenge of Grassroots Environmentalism in the United States," in Bron Raymond Taylor, ed., 1995.

35 Bill Moyers, 1972. *De-Developing the United States though Non-violence* <doingdemocracy.com/De-Developing%20the%20U.S.%20Thru%20Nonviolence.pdf>. (Note: this is Quaker Bill Moyers, not the Bill Moyers of PBS fame.)

36 Bill Moyers and Pamela Haines, *The Progressive*, March 1981.

37 Peter North, *Ecolocalisation as an urban strategy in the context of resource constraint and climate change - a (dangerous) new protectionism?* <extra.shu.ac.uk/ppp-online/issue_1_300409/article_3_full.html>.

38 Patrick Holden <sustainablefoodtrust.org/team/patrick-holden>

39 Richard Heinberg, Foreword to Rob Hopkins, 2008.

40 John Michael Greer, author of *Dark Age America: Climate Change, Cultural Collapse, and the Hard Future Ahead*, 2016.

41 Penny Skerret, Transition City Manchester, personal communication.

42 Timothy Gorringe and Rosie Beckham, 2013.

43 Richard Heinberg, 2011.

44 Rob Hopkins, 2008, 2011, and 2014.

45 Pat Murphy, 2008.

46 Timothy Gorringe and Rosie Beckham, 2013.

47 Hebrew Prayer, North America <greenhearted.org/prayers-for-the-earth.html>

48 Mary Pipher, 2013.

49 Wen Stephenson, 2015.

50 Barbara Kingsolver, 2003.

51 Transition Heathrow <transitionheathrow.com>.

52 Rabbi Arthur Waskow, <theshalomcenter.org/content/prayer-if-earth-really-matters>.

53 Greening Faith <greenfaith.org>.

54 Aldo Leopold, 1974 <eco-action.org/dt/thinking.html>.

55 *Acts* 9:1-9.

56 Thomas Berry, 1988 and 1999.

57 Timothy Gorringe and Rosie Becklam, 2013.

58 Peter Sawtell, Renew Your Church, *Eco-Justice Notes* February 2015, <eco-justice.org/E-100813.asp>.

59 Arthur Waskow, 2014. *We Can't Breathe—An American Travesty.* <theshalom-center.org/content/we-cant-breathe-american-travesty>.

60 Ibrahim Abdul-Matin, 2010.

61 Quran 30:30

62 Quaker Earthcare Witness <quakerearthcare.org>.

63 Hindu Declaration <hinduismtoday.com/pdf_downloads/hindu-climate-change-declaration.pdf>.

64 Ecosikh <ecosikh.org/first-sikh-statement-on-climate-change-presented-by-ecosikh/>.

65 Islam and the Environment: A Global Summit to Spread the Green Message <islam-environment.com/Green%20Message-website%20summary.pdf>.

66 Carolyn Baker, 2011.

67 Starhawk <reclaiming.org/about/directions/unity.html>.

68 George Fox, *Epistle #227, Works.* Philadelphia: Marcus T. Gould, 1831. vol. 7 p.241

69 Tim DeChristopher, 2015, in Wen Stephenson, ed., 2015.

70 Wen Stephenson, 2015.

71 Transition Streets <transitionstreets.org>.

72 KPBS San Diego Public Radio & TV <kpbs.org>.

73 Rob Hopkins, 2015.

74 Steve Chase and Ruah Swennerfelt, *Quaker in Transition* <quakers-in-transition.org>.

75 Rob Hopkins, 2010. Rethinking Transition. *Transition Culture,* June 4, 2010 <transitionnetwork.org/blogs/rob-hopkins>.

76 Naomi Klein, 2014. *The Guardian,* October, 2014. <theguardian.com/membership/video/2014/oct/24/naomi-klein-on-climate-change-and-austerity-video>.

77 Charlotte Du Cann <charlotteducann.blogspot.com>.

78 Bill McKibben, 2015. *New York Times,* December 14, 2015.

79 Lindsey Cook, 2016. *Bring New Narratives to the Climate Negoitiations.* <quakerweb-org.uk/blog/climate-change-2/bringing-new-narrativess-to-the-climate-negotiations>.

80 Greenfaith: Interfaith Partners for the Environment <greenfaith.org>.

81 Midrash Kohelet Rabbah on *Ecclesiastes* 7:13 <jewishvirtuallibrary.org/jsource/judaica/ejud_0002_0006_0_05532.html>.

82 Tikkun 'olam <myjewishlearning.com/article/tikkun-olam-repairing-the-world>.

83 Rob Hopkins, 2015.

84 Transition US *You Know You're in Transition When...* <transitionus.org/stories/you-know-youre-transition-when>.

Bibliography

Abdul-Matin, Ibrahim, 2010. *Green Deen: What Islam Teaches About Protecting the Planet*. San Francisco CA: Berret-Koehler Publishers.

Ackerman-Leist, Philip, 2013. *Rebuilding the Foodshed: How to Create Local, Sustainable, and Secure Food Systems*. Post Carbon Institute. White River Junction VT: Chelsea Green Publishing.

Anderson, Paul, 2013. *Following Jesus*. Newberg OR: Barclay Press.

Baker Carolyn, 2011. *Navigating the Coming Chaos: A Handbook for Inner Transition*. Bloomington IN: iUniverse.

Bane, Peter, 2012. *The Permaculture Handbook*. Gabriola Island, BC: New Society Publishers.

Barlow, Maude, 2002. *Blue Gold: The Battle Against Corporate Theft of the World's Water* (with Tony Clarke). Toronto ON: Stoddart.

Barlow, Maude, 2007. *Blue Covenant: The Global Water Crisis and the Fight for the Right to Water*. Toronto ON: McClelland & Stewart.

Berry, Thomas, 1988. *The Dream of the Earth*. San Francisco CA: Sierra Club Books.

Berry, Thomas, 1999. *The Great Work: The Way into Our Future*. New York NY: Random House.

Boulding, Kenneth, 1964. *The Meaning of the 20th Century: The Great Transition*. New York NY: Harper & Row.

Brooks, Nancy L., 1984. *Dorothy Day and the Quaker Worker*. Albany NY: State of New York Press.

Brown, Peter G., Geoffrey Garver, Keith Helmuth, Robert Howell, Steve Szeghi, 2009. *Right Relationship: Building a Whole Earth Economy*. San Francisco CA: Berrett-Koehler Publishers.

Chamberlin, Shaun, 2009. *The Transition Timeline for a Local, Resilient Future*. White River Junction VT: Chelsea Green Publishing.

Cohen-Kiener, Andrea, 2009. *Claiming Earth as Common Ground: The Ecological Crisis Through the Lens of Faith*. Woodstock VT: Skylight Paths.

Cortese, Amy, 2011. *Locavesting: The Revolution in Local Investing and How to Profit from It*. Hoboken NJ: John Wiley & Sons.

Dreby, Ed, Keith Helmuth, Margaret Mansfield, 2012. *It's the Economy Friends: Understanding the Growth Dilemma*. Quaker Institute for the Future. Caye Caulker, Belize: Producciones de la Hamaca.

Dreby, Ed, and Judy Lumb, eds. 2012. *Beyond the Growth Dilemma: Toward an Ecologically Integrated Economy*. Quaker Institute for the Future. Caye Caulker, Belize: Producciones de la Hamaca.

Flannery, Tim, 2005. *The Weather Makers: How Man is Changing the Climate and What it Means for Life on Earth*. New York NY: Grove Press.

Framarin, Christopher G., 2014. *Hinduism and Environmental Ethics: Law, Literature, and Philosophy*. New York NY: Routledge.

Goodall, Chris, 2007. *How to Live a Low-Carbon Life: The Individual's Guide to Stopping Climate Change*. New York NY: Earthscan.

Gore, Al, 2006. *An Inconvenient Truth: The Crisis of Global Warming.* New York NY: Viking Press.

Gorringe, Timothy, and Rosie Beckham, 2013. *The Transition Movement for Churches: A Prophetic Imperative for Today.* Norwich, UK: Canterbury Press.

Gottlieb, Roger S. 2006. *A Greener Faith: Religious Environmentalism and Our Planet's Future.* New York NY: Oxford University Press.

Greer, John Michael, 2009. *The Ecotechnic Future: Envisioning A Post-Peak World.* Gabriola Island, BC: New Society Publishers.

Gwyn, Douglas, 2014. *A Sustainable Life: Quaker Faith and Practice in the Renewal of Creation.* Philadelphia, PA: FGC Quaker Press.

Hawken, Paul, 2008. *Blessed Unrest: How the Largest Social Movement in History Is Restoring Grace, Justice, and Beauty to the World.* New York NY: Penguin Group.

Heinburg, Richard, 2011. *The End of Growth: Adapting to Our New Economic Reality.* Gabriola Island, BC: New Society Publishers.

Hemenway, Toby, 2000. *Gaia's Garden: A Guide to Home-Scale Permaculture.* White River Junction VT: Chelsea Green Publishing.

Hemenway, Toby, 2015. *The Permaculture City: Regenerative Design for Urban, Suburban, and Town Resilience.* White River Junction VT: Chelsea Green Publishing.

Hewitt, Ben, 2009. *The Town That Food Saved: How One Community Found Vitality in Local Food.* Emmaus, PA: Rodale Books.

Holmgren, David, 2002. *Permaculture: Principles and Pathways Beyond Sustainability.* Hepburn, Victoria, Australia: Holmgren Design Press.

Hopkins, Rob, 2008. *The Transition Handbook: From Oil Dependency to Local Resilience.* White River Junction VT: Chelsea Green Publishing.

Hopkins, Rob, 2011. *The Transition Companion: Making Your Community Resilient in Uncertain Times.* White River Junction VT: Chelsea Green Publishing.

Hopkins, Rob, 2013. *The Power of Just Doing Stuff: How Local Action Can Change the World.* Cambridge, UK: Green Books.

Hopkins, Rob, 2015. *21 Stories of Transition: How a Movement of Communities is Coming Together to Reimagine and Rebuild Our World.* UK: Transition Network.

Kaza, Stephanie, 2008. *Mindfully Green: A Personal and Spiritual Guide to Whole Earth Thinking.* Boulder, CO: Shambhala Publications.

Kingsolver, Barbara, 2003. *Small Wonder.* New York NY: Harper Perennial.

Kleppel, Gary S., 2014. *The Emergent Agriculture: Farming, Sustainability and the Return of the Local Economy.* Gabriola Island, BC: New Society Publishers.

Klein, Naomi, 2014. *This Changes Everything: Capitalism vs. the Climate.* New York NY: Simon & Schuster.

Kolbert, Elizabeth, 2014. *The Sixth Extinction: An Unnatural History.* New York NY: Henry Holt & Co.

Korten, David C., 2001. *When Corporations Rule the World.* San Francisco CA: Berrett-Koehler Publishers.

Korten, David C., 2010. *Agenda for a New Economy: From Phantom Wealth to Real Wealth*. San Francisco CA: Berrett-Koehler Publishers.

Leopold, Aldo, 1949. *A Sand County Almanac*. New York NY: Oxford University Press.

Macy, Joanna, 2007. *World as Lover, World As Self: Courage for Global Justice and Ecological Renewal*. Berkeley CA: Parallax Press.

Macy, Joanna and Molly Brown, 2014. *Coming Back to Life. The Updated Guide to the Work that Reconnects*. Gabriola Island, BC: New Society Publishers.

McKibben, Bill, 1989. *The End of Nature*. New York NY: Random House.

McKibben, Bill, 2005. *The Comforting Whirlwind: God, Job, and the Scale of Creation*. Cambridge MA: Cowley Publications.

Meadows, Donella, Jorgen Randers, Dennis Meadows, 2004. *Limits to Growth: the 30-Year Update*. White River Junction VT: Chelsea Green Publishing.

Meeker-Lowry, Susan, 1988. *Economics As If the Earth Really Mattered: A Catalyst Guide to Socially Conscious Investing*. Gabriola Island, BC: New Society Publishers.

Monbiot, George, 2007. *Heat: How to Stop the Planet from Burning*. New York NY: Penguin Books.

Moore, Kathleen Dean, and Michael P. Nelson, eds., 2010. *Moral Ground: Ethical Action for a Planet in Peril*. San Antonio TX: Trinity University Press.

Murphy, Pat, 2008. *Plan C*. Gabriola Island, BC: New Society Publishers.

Pipher, Mary, 2013. *The Green Boat: Reviving Ourselves in Our Capsized Culture*. New York NY: Riverhead Books.

Pollan, Michael, 2006. *The Omnivore's Dilemma: A Natural History of Four Meals*. New York NY: Penguin Books.

Pope Francis, 2015. *On Care for Our Common Home: (Laudato SI')*. Washington DC: United States Conference of Bishops.

Quammen, David, 1996: *The Song of the Dodo: Island Biogeography in an Age of Extinction*. New York NY: Touchstone.

Robin, Vicki, 2014. *Blessing the Hands That Feed Us: What Eating Closer to Home Can Teach Us About Food, Community, and Our Place on Earth*. New York NY: Viking Press.

Seidl, Amy, 2011. *Finding Higher Ground: Adaptation in the Age of Warming*. Boston MA: Beacon Press.

Starhawk, 1987. *Truth or Dare: Encounters with Power, Authority, and Mystery*. San Francisco CA: Harper.

Starhawk, 1993. *The Fifth Sacred Thing*. New York NY: Bantam.

Starhawk, 2011. *The Empowerment Manual: A Guide for Collaborative Groups*. Gabriola Island, BC: New Society Publishers.

Stephenson, Wen, 2015. *What We're Fighting for Now is Each Other: Dispatches from the Front Lines of Climate Justice*. Boston MA: Beacon Press.

Tasch, Woody, 2011. *Inquiries into the Nature of Slow Money: Investing as if Food, Farms, and Fertility Mattered*. White River Junction VT: Chelsea Green Publishing.

Taylor, Bron Raymond, ed. 1995. *Ecological Resistance Movements: The Global Emergence of Radical and Popular Environmentalism.* Albany NY: State University of New York Press.

Tokar, Brian, 1999. *Earth for Sale: Reclaiming Ecology in the Age of Corporate Greenwash.* Boston MA: Southend Press.

Tokar, Brian, 2004. *Gene Traders: Biotechnology, World Trade, and the Globalization of Hunger.* Burlington VT: Toward Freedom.

Tokar, Brian, 2014. *Toward Climate Justice: Perspectives on the Climate Crisis and Social Change.* Porsgrunn, Norway: New Compass Press.

Mark Wallace, 2010. *Green Christianity: Five Ways to a Sustainable Future.* Minneapolis MN: Augsburg Fortress.

Waskow, Arthur O., 1995. *Down-to-Earth Judaism.* New York NY: William Morrow Publishing.

Waskow, Arthur O., 1996. *Godwrestling — Round 2.* Woodstock VT: Jewish Lights Publishing.

Waskow, Arthur O., ed., 2000. *Torah of the Earth.* Woodstock VT: Jewish Lights Publishing.

Waskow, Arthur O. with Ari Elon & Naomi Mara Hyman, eds., 1999. *Trees, Earth, and Torah.* Philadelphia PA: Jewish Publication Society.

Waskow, Arthur O. and Phyllis O. Berman, 2011. *Freedom Journeys: The Tale of Exodus and Wilderness Across Millennia.* Woodstock VT: Jewish Lights Publishing.

de Weyer, Robert Van, 2003. *366 Readings from Islam.* Ottawa ON: Laurier Books Ltd.

Yes! Magazine, Bainbridge Island WA <yesmagazine.org>.

Films

Ankele, John, and Anne Macksoud, Directors; Michael Sacca, Videography; and Eugene Friesen, Music. *Wisdom to Survive: Capitalism, Climate Change, and Community.* Oley, PA: Bullfrog Films <bullfrogfilms.com/catalog/wts.html>.

Bright Blue Ecomedia, 2015. *The Resilient Ones: A Generation Takes on Climate Change.* <brightbluemedia.org>.

Garcia, Debora Koons, 2004. *The Future of Food.* Lily Films <thefutureoffood.com>.

Goude, Emma Producer, animation by Emilio Mula, photography by Beccy Strong and music by Rebecca Mayes. *In Transition 2.0.* Green Lane Films. Available in DVD or on YouTube <transitionnetwork.org/transition-2>.

Kenner, Robert, 2014. *Merchants of Doubt* <sonyclassics.com/merchantsofdoubt>.

Ostrow, Marty and Terry Kay Rockefeller, 2007. *Renewal.* Fine Cut Productions <renewalproject.net>.

Tucker, Mary Evelyn, and Brian Thomas Swimme, 2011. *Journey of the Universe.* <journeyoftheuniverse.org>.

List of Interviews

Anton Adreasson, Alingsås, Sweden, June 21, 2011

Murad Al Kufash, Marda, Palestine, May 6, 2011

Rabbi Katy Allen, Wayland, Massachusetts, February 9, 2015

Carolyn Baker, Boulder, Colorado, November 12, 2014

Ron Berezan, Powell River, British Columbia, November 10, 2014 (by email)

Pierre Bertrand, Trieves, France, June 4, 2011

Ralph Boehlke, Paris, France, June 4, 2011

Olivier Bori, Tervuren, Belgium, June 18, 2011

Cristiano Bottone, Monteveglio, Italy, May 24, 2011

Steve Chase, Wallingsford, Pennsylvania, June - July, 2014 (by email)

Maggie Flemming, Sebastopol, California, October 28, 2014 (by email)

Paul Flynn, Tramore, Ireland, June 9, 2014

Naresh Giangrande, Totnes, England, June 4, 2011

Massimo Giorgini, Monteveglio, Italy, May 24, 2011

Rob Hopkins, Totnes, England, July 10, 2011

Marc Van Hummelen, Tervuren, Belgium, June 18, 2011

Prerana (Rani) Jayakumar, Palo Alto, California, October 28, 2014 (by email)

Jeremy Light, Trieves, France, June 4, 2011

Isabela de Menezes, Liverpool, England, July 10, 2014

Phil Metzler, interview by telephone, November 8, 2014

Silvia Neri, Monteveglio, Italy, May 24, 2011

George Owen, Media, Pennsylvania, April 5, 2011

Joanne Poyourow, Los Angeles, California, October 26, 2011

Isobel Vandermeulen, Tervuren, Belgium, June 18, 2011

Ruah Swennerfelt
(*photo by Lelia Brooke Hagerman*)

Ruah Swennerfelt is a founding member of Transition Town Charlotte and a member of Burlington Friends Meeting (Quakers) in Vermont, USA. She served as General Secretary for Quaker Earthcare Witness (QEW) for 17 years. During her tenure with QEW she helped Friends and Friends Meetings to become aware of the spiritual relationship that humans have with Earth and to make changes in their lives that would bring them more in harmony with that relationship. After leaving her work at QEW, Ruah traveled in Israel, Europe, and parts of the United States interviewing people involved in Transition and visiting their Initiatives. Much of what she learned from those visits inspired the writing of this book.

Ruah currently serves as president of the Transition Town Charlotte board, serves on the Transition US Collaborative Design Council, and as clerk of the New England Yearly Meeting Earthcare Ministry Committee. She has given many presentations, workshops, and keynote talks across North America and in England. She has written numerous articles for *BeFriending Creation, Friends Journal,* and *Quaker Life*. She has authored and co-authored chapters in several books. She blogs at <transitionvision.org>.

She and her husband, Louis Cox, live in rural Vermont where they grow most of their vegetables and fruits, make their own electricity and heat their water from the sun, attempting to live lives that are simple, rich, and meaningful.

QUAKER INSTITUTE FOR THE FUTURE

Advancing a global future of inclusion,
social justice, and ecological integrity through
participatory research and discernment.

The Quaker Institute for the Future (QIF) seeks to generate systematic insight, knowledge, and wisdom that can inform public policy and enable us to treat all humans, all communities of life, and the whole Earth as manifestations of the Divine. QIF creates the opportunity for Quaker scholars and practitioners to apply the social and ecological intelligence of their disciplines within the context of Friends' testimonies and the Quaker traditions of truth seeking and public service.

The focus of the Institute's concerns include:

- Moving from economic policies and practices that undermine Earth's capacity to support life to an ecologically based economy that works for the security, vitality and resilience of human communities and the well-being of the entire commonwealth of planetary life.

- Bringing the governance of the common good into the regulation of technologies that holds us responsible for the future well-being of humanity and the Earth.

- Reducing structural violence arising from economic privilege, social exclusion, and environmental degradation through the expansion of equitable sharing, inclusion, justice, and ecosystem restoration.

- Reversing the growing segregation of people into enclaves of privilege and deprivation through public policies and public trust institutions that facilitate equity of access to the means life.

- Engaging the complexity of global interdependence and its demands on governance systems, institutional accountability, and citizen's responsibilities.

- Moving from societal norms of aggressive individualism, winner-take-all competition, and economic aggrandizement to the practices of cooperation, collaboration, commonwealth sharing, and an economy keyed to strengthening the common good.